THE PSYCHOLOGICAL AND EMOTIONAL IMPACT OF RESTORATIVE JUSTICE

Dr. Maxwell Shimba

Printed by Shimba Publishing LLC
Printed in the United States of America

TABLE OF CONTENTS

INTRODUCTION

Restorative justice is more than just a legal approach; it is a transformative way of addressing harm that centers on healing, accountability, and community well-being. In traditional justice systems, the focus tends to be on punishment—ensuring that offenders are penalized for their wrongdoing. However, this punitive approach often overlooks the emotional and psychological needs of both victims and offenders, leaving deep scars that continue to affect individuals and communities long after the legal process is complete. The Psychological and Emotional Impact of Restorative Justice by Dr. Maxwell Shimba offers an in-depth exploration of how restorative justice presents an alternative framework that prioritizes emotional healing, empathy, and long-term reconciliation.

This book delves into the psychological and emotional dynamics that shape restorative justice, emphasizing the human experience at its core. By examining the emotional needs of victims, the accountability and transformation of offenders, and the broader implications for communities, restorative justice presents a unique opportunity to heal harm in a way that the traditional justice system often fails to achieve. Through restorative practices, victims gain a voice and the opportunity to seek closure, offenders confront the impact of their actions, and communities are given the chance to rebuild trust and social cohesion. Restorative justice is not just about resolving a conflict but about restoring the emotional and social fabric that has been torn apart by crime or harm.

This book is divided into multiple chapters that systematically address the key components of restorative justice, offering both theoretical foundations and practical applications. From understanding the historical context and principles of restorative justice to examining the psychological theories that support it, this work seeks to provide a comprehensive framework for understanding its emotional and psychological impacts. Through case studies, empirical data, and personal narratives, Dr. Shimba brings to light the profound ways in which restorative justice reshapes the lives of those involved. Whether you are a scholar, practitioner, or someone interested in justice reform, The Psychological and Emotional Impact of Restorative Justice offers valuable insights into a justice model that not only repairs harm but also fosters deeper emotional healing and social transformation.

DR. MAXWELL SHIMBA

CHAPTER 01

INTRODUCTION TO THE PSYCHOLOGICAL AND EMOTIONAL IMPACTS OF RESTORATIVE JUSTICE

Restorative justice represents a transformative approach to addressing crime and conflict, focusing on healing and reconciliation rather than punishment. This book aims to delve into the psychological and emotional impacts of restorative justice on all participants involved—victims, offenders, and the broader community. By examining the benefits and potential risks, we hope to provide a comprehensive understanding of how restorative justice circles can contribute to personal and communal healing.

The Concept of Restorative Justice

Restorative justice is rooted in the belief that crime causes harm to people and relationships, and justice should aim to repair that harm. Unlike the traditional retributive justice system, which emphasizes punishment, restorative justice seeks to bring together all parties affected by a crime to collaboratively decide on a path forward that promotes healing and resolution.

Historical Background

Restorative justice has ancient roots, drawing from indigenous practices around the world that emphasized community involvement and collective healing. Over the past few decades, it has gained renewed attention and has been increasingly incorporated into modern justice systems as an alternative or complementary approach.

Objectives of This Book

The primary objectives of this book are to:

1. Explore the Psychological Impact: Investigate how restorative justice affects the mental health and psychological well-being of victims, offenders, and community members.

2. Examine the Emotional Effects: Understand the range of emotional responses elicited by participation in restorative justice processes, including both positive outcomes and potential emotional risks.

3. Highlight Benefits: Discuss the numerous benefits of restorative justice, such as increased empathy, reduced recidivism, and the fostering of community cohesion.

4. Address Challenges: Identify and analyze the potential challenges and risks associated with restorative justice, providing strategies to mitigate these issues.

5. Provide Practical Guidance: Offer best practices for implementing restorative justice, including training for facilitators and case studies that illustrate successful applications.

Importance of Understanding Psychological and Emotional Impacts

Understanding the psychological and emotional impacts of restorative justice is crucial for several reasons:

- Enhancing Effectiveness: By recognizing how restorative justice affects participants, programs can be tailored to maximize positive outcomes and address potential pitfalls.

- Supporting Participants: Knowledge of psychological and emotional impacts allows for better support of all participants, ensuring that their needs are met throughout the process.

- Promoting Widespread Adoption: Demonstrating the benefits and addressing the challenges of restorative justice can encourage its broader adoption within justice systems and communities.

Structure of the Book

This book is organized into ten chapters, each focusing on different aspects of restorative justice:

1. Introduction: An overview of restorative justice and the goals of this book.

2. Understanding Restorative Justice: Definitions, principles, and historical context.

3. Psychological Foundations: Theories of justice and psychological principles relevant to restorative justice.

4. Emotional Effects: Detailed examination of the emotional impacts on victims, offenders, and community members.

5. Benefits: Exploration of the key benefits of restorative justice, including empathy, healing, and reduced recidivism.

6. Risks and Challenges: Analysis of potential risks and challenges, and how to address them.

7. Implementing Restorative Justice: Best practices, case studies, and training for facilitators.

8. Measuring Impact: Methods for assessing the impact of restorative justice, including qualitative and quantitative measures.

9. Future Directions: Policy recommendations and integration with traditional justice systems.

10. Conclusion: Summary of key points and final reflections.

Restorative justice offers a powerful alternative to traditional punitive approaches, emphasizing healing and reconciliation. By delving into the psychological and emotional impacts of restorative justice, this book aims to provide valuable insights and practical guidance for those involved in or considering the implementation of restorative justice practices. Through a comprehensive examination of both the benefits and challenges, we hope to contribute to the ongoing evolution and effectiveness of restorative justice in promoting personal and communal well-being.

The Concept of Restorative Justice

Restorative justice is an innovative approach to addressing crime and conflict that shifts the focus from punishment to healing and reconciliation. Rooted in ancient traditions and adapted for modern use, restorative justice emphasizes the repair of harm and the restoration of relationships rather than the retributive model that seeks to penalize the offender. This chapter explores the fundamental principles, historical context, and practical applications of restorative justice, providing a comprehensive understanding of its concept.

Fundamental Principles of Restorative Justice

At its core, restorative justice is built on several key principles that guide its practice and distinguish it from traditional justice systems:

1. Repairing Harm: Restorative justice acknowledges that crime causes harm to individuals, relationships, and communities. The primary goal is to repair this harm to the greatest extent possible. This involves addressing the needs of victims, holding offenders accountable in a constructive manner, and engaging the community in the healing process.

2. Inclusive Decision-Making: A hallmark of restorative justice is the inclusion of all stakeholders—victims, offenders, and community members—in the decision-making process. This collaborative approach ensures that all voices are heard and that solutions are mutually agreed upon, fostering a sense of ownership and commitment to the outcomes.

3. Accountability and Responsibility: Restorative justice emphasizes the importance of offenders taking responsibility for their actions and understanding the impact of their behavior on others. This accountability is seen as a crucial step in the offender's rehabilitation and reintegration into the community.

4. Reintegration: Unlike punitive systems that often stigmatize and isolate offenders, restorative justice seeks to reintegrate them into society as productive and valued members. This involves providing support and opportunities for personal growth and development, reducing the likelihood of reoffending.

5. Voluntary Participation: Participation in restorative justice processes is typically voluntary. All parties must willingly engage in the process, ensuring that it is a genuine and respectful dialogue rather than a coercive or adversarial encounter.

Historical Context and Evolution

Restorative justice has deep historical roots, drawing from indigenous practices around the world that emphasized communal healing and conflict resolution. Indigenous cultures in Africa, North America, and New Zealand, among others, have long practiced forms of restorative justice, where the community plays a central role in addressing wrongdoing and restoring harmony.

In modern times, restorative justice began to gain formal recognition and development in the 1970s and 1980s. The movement was partly a response to the perceived failures of the retributive justice system, which often left victims feeling neglected and offenders unrehabilitated. Early restorative justice programs focused on victim-offender mediation and gradually expanded to include various models such as family group conferencing, peacemaking circles, and restorative justice panels.

Models of Restorative Justice

Restorative justice can be implemented through various models, each tailored to the specific context and needs of the participants. Some of the most common models include:

1. Victim-Offender Mediation: This model involves direct dialogue between the victim and the offender, facilitated by a trained mediator. The goal is to allow the victim to express the impact of the crime, and for the offender to acknowledge their actions and work towards restitution and resolution.

2. Family Group Conferencing: Originating in New Zealand, this model brings together the victim, offender, their families, and other supporters in a structured meeting. The group collaboratively develops a plan to address the harm caused and to support the offender's reintegration.

3. Peacemaking Circles: Rooted in indigenous traditions, peacemaking circles involve a broader community gathering where participants sit in a circle and use a talking piece to ensure respectful and egalitarian dialogue. The process fosters mutual understanding and collective decision-making.

4. Restorative Justice Panels: These panels, often composed of community volunteers, meet with offenders to discuss the crime and its impact. The panel and the offender

work together to develop a restitution plan that addresses the needs of the victim and the community.

Benefits of Restorative Justice

Restorative justice offers numerous benefits for victims, offenders, and communities, making it an appealing alternative to traditional punitive systems:

1. For Victims:

- Empowerment: Victims have the opportunity to share their stories and express their needs, often leading to a greater sense of empowerment and closure.

- Healing: By participating in the restorative process, victims can experience emotional healing and a sense of justice that acknowledges their pain and suffering.

2. For Offenders:

- Accountability: Offenders are encouraged to take responsibility for their actions and to understand the impact of their behavior on others, which is a crucial step towards rehabilitation.

- Rehabilitation: Restorative justice provides a supportive environment for offenders to make amends and to develop positive relationships with the community.

3. For Communities:

- Cohesion: Restorative justice fosters community involvement and collective problem-solving, strengthening social bonds and enhancing community cohesion.

- Safety: By addressing the underlying causes of crime and supporting the reintegration of offenders, restorative justice can contribute to long-term community safety.

Challenges and Criticisms

Despite its many benefits, restorative justice also faces several challenges and criticisms that must be addressed to ensure its effectiveness and fairness:

1. Power Imbalances: Ensuring that all participants have an equal voice in the process can be challenging, especially in cases involving significant power imbalances between victims and offenders.

2. Voluntariness: The voluntary nature of restorative justice means that it may not be appropriate or effective in all cases, particularly if one party is unwilling to participate genuinely.

3. Consistency and Training: Implementing restorative justice requires well-trained facilitators and consistent practices to ensure that the process is conducted fairly and effectively.

4. Integration with Traditional Justice Systems: Balancing restorative justice with traditional punitive systems

can be complex, requiring careful consideration of how the two approaches can complement each other.

Restorative justice represents a transformative approach to addressing crime and conflict, emphasizing healing, accountability, and community involvement. By focusing on repairing harm and restoring relationships, restorative justice offers a powerful alternative to retributive justice systems that often fail to meet the needs of victims, offenders, and communities. As this chapter has explored, the concept of restorative justice is rooted in ancient traditions and has evolved into a modern practice with significant psychological and emotional benefits. Understanding its principles, models, and potential challenges is crucial for those seeking to implement or participate in restorative justice processes, paving the way for a more compassionate and effective approach to justice.

Historical Background

Restorative justice, as a concept and practice, has deep and ancient roots. Drawing from indigenous traditions and evolving through the centuries, restorative justice has emerged as a significant alternative and complement to modern retributive justice systems. This chapter delves into the historical background of restorative justice, exploring its origins, evolution, and contemporary resurgence.

Indigenous Roots

Indigenous Practices in North America

Among the Native American tribes, restorative practices were deeply embedded in their cultural traditions. The concept of justice was intertwined with the health and harmony of the community. For example, the Navajo Nation has long utilized peacemaking practices, which focus on restoring relationships and community well-being rather than simply punishing the offender. In these communities, justice was seen as a process of healing and reconciliation, involving not just the victim and the offender, but the entire community.

African Traditions

In Africa, restorative justice practices have been a cornerstone of community life for centuries. The concept of Ubuntu, which emphasizes humanity, compassion, and interconnectedness, plays a central role in justice practices across many African cultures. In Rwanda, the Gacaca courts were a traditional form of community justice that focused on truth-telling, accountability, and reconciliation. These courts were revitalized after the 1994 genocide to facilitate healing and rebuild the social fabric of the nation.

Maori Traditions in New Zealand

The Maori people of New Zealand have a long history of restorative justice practices, known as Whanau Conferencing. These practices are deeply rooted in Maori values of collective responsibility and the restoration of harmony. The principles of Whanau Conferencing have significantly influenced modern restorative justice programs, particularly the Family Group Conferencing model, which has been adopted in various parts of the world.

Early Modern Influences

Quaker Contributions

In the 17th century, the Quakers in England and North America introduced restorative principles into their justice practices. The Quakers believed in the inherent worth of every individual and emphasized reconciliation and forgiveness. Their influence can be seen in the development of the penitentiary system, which was initially intended to be a place for reflection and penance rather than mere punishment.

19th and 20th Century Reform Movements

Throughout the 19th and 20th centuries, various reform movements began to challenge the efficacy and humanity of punitive justice systems. The juvenile justice reform movement, for example, emphasized rehabilitation over punishment and laid the groundwork for restorative practices. Progressive reformers advocated for a justice system that considered the social and psychological needs of offenders and victims alike.

Contemporary Resurgence

The 1970s and 1980s: A Turning Point

The modern restorative justice movement gained significant momentum in the 1970s and 1980s. During this period, dissatisfaction with the traditional criminal justice system grew, driven by high recidivism rates, the marginalization of victims, and the recognition of the system's failure to address the root causes of crime.

In 1974, the first modern victim-offender reconciliation program (VORP) was established in Kitchener, Ontario, Canada. This program brought together victims and offenders to discuss the impact of the crime and agree on a plan for restitution. The success of this program sparked interest and the development of similar initiatives worldwide.

International Adoption and Adaptation

Restorative justice principles began to be incorporated into national and international justice systems during the late 20th and early 21st centuries. Countries such as New Zealand, Australia, Canada, and the United Kingdom developed restorative justice programs within their criminal justice systems. These programs included victim-offender mediation, family group conferencing, and peacemaking circles.

The United Nations also played a crucial role in promoting restorative justice. In 2002, the UN adopted the Basic Principles on the Use of Restorative Justice Programmes in Criminal Matters, encouraging member states to integrate restorative practices into their justice systems.

Key Historical Milestones

The Development of Family Group Conferencing

Inspired by Maori traditions, New Zealand introduced Family Group Conferencing (FGC) into its juvenile justice system in the late 1980s. This approach brought together the offender, the victim, their families, and other community members to collectively decide on a resolution. FGC has since been adopted in various countries and has significantly influenced the development of restorative justice practices.

The Gacaca Courts in Rwanda

After the 1994 genocide, Rwanda faced the monumental task of achieving justice and reconciliation. The Gacaca courts, a traditional form of community justice, were revived to address the vast number of genocide cases. These courts focused on truth-telling, accountability, and community healing. While not without criticism, the Gacaca courts played a vital role in Rwanda's recovery and highlighted the potential of restorative justice in post-conflict settings.

The Rise of Restorative Practices in Schools

In the late 20th and early 21st centuries, restorative practices began to be implemented in educational settings as a way to address conflict, reduce disciplinary issues, and build positive school climates. Schools in the United States, the United Kingdom, and other countries have adopted restorative practices, such as restorative circles and peer mediation, to promote empathy, accountability, and community among students.

The Evolution of Restorative Justice in the 21st Century

Integration with Traditional Justice Systems

The 21st century has seen increasing efforts to integrate restorative justice with traditional justice systems. Hybrid models have emerged, where restorative practices complement retributive measures, providing a more holistic approach to justice. For example, some jurisdictions use restorative justice as a diversionary tactic for certain offenses, allowing offenders to avoid formal prosecution by participating in restorative processes.

Expanding Applications

Restorative justice has expanded beyond criminal justice to address conflicts in various contexts, including schools, workplaces, and communities. This broader application underscores the versatility and effectiveness of restorative principles in promoting healing and resolution across different settings.

Ongoing Research and Development

The field of restorative justice continues to evolve, with ongoing research and development aimed at refining practices, measuring outcomes, and addressing challenges. Academic institutions, non-profit organizations, and governmental bodies collaborate to study the impacts of restorative justice and to develop best practices for its implementation.

The historical background of restorative justice reveals a rich tapestry of traditions, influences, and innovations that have shaped its development. From its indigenous roots to its modern resurgence, restorative justice has consistently emphasized the importance of healing, accountability, and community involvement. As we move forward, understanding this history is crucial for appreciating the depth and potential of restorative justice as a transformative approach to addressing crime and conflict. Through continued exploration and application, restorative justice holds the promise of fostering more compassionate, effective, and equitable justice systems worldwide.

Explore the Psychological Impact

The psychological impact of restorative justice is profound and multifaceted, affecting victims, offenders, and community members in unique and transformative ways. Unlike traditional retributive justice systems that often leave psychological wounds unaddressed, restorative justice aims to heal these wounds through empathy, accountability, and communal support. This chapter delves into the psychological dimensions of restorative justice, exploring its effects on mental health and psychological well-being for all participants involved.

Psychological Impact on Victims

Empowerment and Voice

One of the most significant psychological benefits for victims participating in restorative justice is the sense of empowerment and the opportunity to have their voices heard. Traditional justice systems often marginalize victims, focusing primarily on punishing the offender. In contrast, restorative justice centers the victim's experience, allowing them to express their emotions, describe the impact of the crime, and participate actively in the resolution process.

- Expression of Emotions: Victims are given a platform to share their stories and feelings, which can be cathartic and validating. This process helps in alleviating feelings of helplessness and frustration.

- Sense of Control: By involving victims in decision-making, restorative justice restores a sense of control over their lives, contributing to psychological empowerment.

Healing and Closure

Restorative justice facilitates emotional healing and closure for victims. The process of confronting the offender and engaging in a dialogue about the crime can lead to:

- Reduced Anxiety and Fear: Understanding the reasons behind the offender's actions and receiving an apology can help reduce anxiety and fear associated with the crime.

- Emotional Release: The opportunity to express anger, sadness, and other emotions in a safe and supportive environment aids in emotional release and healing.

Restitution and Reparation

Restitution agreements reached through restorative justice can provide tangible and psychological benefits to victims. Knowing that the offender is making amends and taking responsibility for their actions can foster a sense of justice and fairness, aiding in the recovery process.

Psychological Impact on Offenders

Accountability and Self-Reflection

Restorative justice requires offenders to confront the consequences of their actions, promoting self-reflection and accountability. This process is crucial for psychological growth and rehabilitation.

- Understanding Impact: Offenders gain insight into the harm they have caused, which can lead to genuine remorse and a desire to make amends.

- Personal Growth: The experience of taking responsibility and participating in restorative processes can contribute to personal development and a reformed identity.

Reduction in Recidivism

Engaging in restorative justice has been linked to lower recidivism rates among offenders. The psychological mechanisms behind this reduction include:

- Increased Empathy: Offenders develop greater empathy for their victims and the community, reducing the likelihood of reoffending.

- Positive Reintegration: The supportive and non-punitive nature of restorative justice facilitates positive reintegration into society, reducing feelings of alienation and promoting prosocial behavior.

Psychological Relief

Offenders often experience psychological relief and reduced guilt through restorative justice. The opportunity to apologize and make amends can alleviate the burden of guilt and shame, contributing to emotional well-being.

Psychological Impact on Community Members

Community Cohesion and Trust

Restorative justice involves the community in the healing process, strengthening social bonds and fostering trust. This communal approach has several psychological benefits:

- Collective Responsibility: Community members develop a sense of collective responsibility and involvement in maintaining social harmony.

- Enhanced Trust: Participating in restorative justice processes enhances trust among community members, creating a supportive and cohesive environment.

Shared Healing and Empathy

The communal nature of restorative justice promotes shared healing and empathy. Community members who witness or participate in restorative justice circles often experience:

- Increased Empathy: Exposure to the experiences and emotions of victims and offenders fosters empathy and understanding among community members.

- Healing Through Support: The act of supporting victims and offenders through the restorative process contributes to communal healing and resilience.

Active Participation in Justice

Restorative justice empowers community members to play an active role in the justice process, which can enhance their psychological well-being.

- Sense of Agency: Community members feel a sense of agency and involvement in addressing crime and promoting justice.

- Satisfaction with Justice Outcomes: Participating in the process can lead to greater satisfaction with justice outcomes, as community members see tangible results and positive changes.

Challenges and Considerations

While the psychological benefits of restorative justice are significant, it is essential to address potential challenges and considerations to ensure the well-being of all participants.

Emotional Risks for Victims

- Re-traumatization: Victims may experience re-traumatization when confronting offenders or recounting their experiences. It is crucial to provide adequate support and preparation to mitigate this risk.

- Expectations Management: Ensuring that victims have realistic expectations about the outcomes of restorative justice processes is vital for their psychological well-being.

Emotional Risks for Offenders

- Shame and Guilt: While acknowledging harm is essential, excessive shame and guilt can be detrimental. Facilitators must balance accountability with support to prevent negative psychological impacts.

- Social Stigma: Offenders may continue to face social stigma even after participating in restorative justice, which can hinder their reintegration and psychological recovery.

Facilitator Training and Support

- Skilled Facilitation: Effective restorative justice requires skilled facilitators who can navigate complex emotions and power dynamics. Proper training and support for facilitators are essential.

- Ongoing Support: Providing ongoing psychological support for all participants, including facilitators, ensures that the restorative process remains beneficial and sustainable.

Exploring the psychological impact of restorative justice reveals its potential to transform the lives of victims, offenders, and community members. By emphasizing healing, accountability, and communal support, restorative justice addresses the emotional and psychological dimensions of crime and conflict that traditional justice systems often overlook. Understanding these impacts is crucial for implementing effective restorative justice practices that promote mental health and well-being for all involved. As this book continues to explore the various facets of restorative justice, the insights gained from examining its psychological impact will serve as a foundation for understanding its broader benefits and challenges.

Examine the Emotional Effects of Restorative Justice

Restorative justice, by its very nature, deeply engages the emotional lives of its participants. This approach to justice focuses on healing and reconciliation, requiring a level of emotional involvement that traditional retributive justice often lacks. The emotional responses elicited through restorative justice processes are diverse, encompassing both positive outcomes and potential risks. This chapter aims to comprehensively examine these emotional effects on victims, offenders, and community members, highlighting the transformative power of restorative justice as well as its challenges.

Emotional Effects on Victims

Positive Emotional Outcomes

1. Empowerment and Validation:

- Voice and Agency: Restorative justice processes give victims a platform to voice their experiences and feelings, which can lead to a sense of empowerment. Being heard and validated is crucial for emotional healing.

- Restoration of Control: By participating actively in the justice process, victims regain a sense of control over their lives, countering the helplessness often caused by the crime.

2. Emotional Healing and Closure:

- Emotional Release: Sharing their story and confronting the offender can provide victims with an emotional release, helping them to process and move past their trauma.

- Forgiveness and Reconciliation: While not all victims reach forgiveness, many find peace through understanding the offender's perspective and receiving an apology.

3. Psychological Relief:

- Reduction in Fear and Anxiety: Understanding the circumstances of the crime and hearing the offender's remorse can alleviate fears and anxieties related to the incident.

- Sense of Justice: Knowing that the offender is taking responsibility and making amends can satisfy the victim's need for justice and fairness.

Potential Emotional Risks

1. Re-traumatization:

- Reliving the Trauma: The process of recounting the crime and facing the offender can sometimes re-trigger traumatic memories, causing emotional distress.

- Emotional Overwhelm: The intensity of the emotions involved may be overwhelming for some victims, leading to additional psychological strain.

2. Disappointment and Frustration:

- Unmet Expectations: If the restorative process does not meet the victim's expectations, it can lead to feelings of disappointment and frustration.

- Perceived Insincerity: If the victim perceives the offender's remorse or apology as insincere, it can exacerbate feelings of anger and betrayal.

Emotional Effects on Offenders

Positive Emotional Outcomes

1. Accountability and Remorse:

- Genuine Remorse: Engaging with the victim and understanding the impact of their actions can foster genuine remorse in offenders.

- Personal Accountability: The process encourages offenders to take responsibility for their actions, which is a critical step towards rehabilitation.

2. Personal Growth and Transformation:

- Empathy Development: Offenders often develop greater empathy as they hear the victim's story and recognize the harm they have caused.

- Positive Identity Change: Through the restorative process, offenders can begin to see themselves as capable of change and improvement, fostering a more positive self-identity.

3. Psychological Relief:

- Alleviation of Guilt: Taking responsibility and making amends can relieve feelings of guilt and shame, contributing to emotional well-being.

- Sense of Redemption: Participating in restorative justice can provide a path to redemption, helping offenders to reintegrate into society with a renewed sense of purpose.

Potential Emotional Risks

1. Shame and Stigma:

- Intense Shame: While some level of shame is necessary for accountability, excessive shame can be detrimental, leading to feelings of worthlessness and despair.

- Social Stigma: Even after participating in restorative justice, offenders may continue to face social stigma, which can hinder their emotional and psychological recovery.

2. Emotional Vulnerability:

- Exposure of Emotions: The restorative process requires offenders to be emotionally vulnerable, which can be challenging and uncomfortable.

- Fear of Rejection: Offenders may fear rejection by the victim and the community, causing anxiety and emotional distress.

Emotional Effects on Community Members

Positive Emotional Outcomes

1. Enhanced Empathy and Compassion:

- Increased Understanding: Witnessing the restorative process fosters empathy and compassion among community members, as they gain a deeper understanding of both the victim's and the offender's experiences.

- Collective Healing: The community's involvement in the healing process promotes a sense of collective responsibility and solidarity.

2. Community Cohesion and Trust:

- Strengthened Bonds: Restorative justice processes can strengthen social bonds and enhance trust within the community.

- Shared Responsibility: Engaging in the justice process fosters a sense of shared responsibility for maintaining peace and harmony.

3. Active Participation and Agency:

- Sense of Involvement: Community members who participate in restorative justice feel more involved and empowered in addressing crime and conflict.

- Positive Community Identity: The collective effort to restore justice and harmony contributes to a positive community identity.

Potential Emotional Risks

1. Emotional Burden:

- Vicarious Trauma: Community members may experience vicarious trauma from hearing about and engaging with the emotional experiences of victims and offenders.

- Emotional Exhaustion: The emotional intensity of restorative justice processes can lead to burnout or emotional exhaustion for community members involved.

2. Conflict and Tension:

- Diverse Perspectives: Differences in opinion about the restorative process or its outcomes can cause conflict and tension within the community.

- Managing Expectations: Balancing the diverse expectations and needs of all participants can be challenging and emotionally taxing.

Facilitator's Role in Managing Emotional Effects

Emotional Intelligence and Skills

Effective facilitators play a crucial role in managing the emotional dynamics of restorative justice processes. Key skills include:

- Emotional Intelligence: Facilitators must possess high emotional intelligence to navigate complex emotional landscapes and support participants effectively.

- Active Listening: Skilled facilitators practice active listening, validating participants' emotions and fostering a safe and supportive environment.

Preparation and Support

Proper preparation and ongoing support are essential for managing the emotional effects of restorative justice:

- Pre-Process Preparation: Facilitators should prepare participants for the emotional journey ahead, setting realistic expectations and providing coping strategies.

- Ongoing Support: Continuous emotional support should be available to all participants, ensuring they feel supported throughout and after the process.

Understanding the emotional effects of restorative justice is vital for maximizing its benefits and addressing its challenges. By examining the range of emotional responses elicited in victims, offenders, and community members, this chapter highlights both the transformative power and the potential risks of restorative justice processes. Recognizing these emotional dynamics and providing adequate support can ensure that restorative justice fosters healing, empathy, and reconciliation, ultimately contributing to more compassionate and effective justice systems. As we continue to explore the facets of restorative justice, the insights gained from examining its emotional impacts will be foundational for understanding its broader implications and applications.

Highlight Benefits

Restorative justice offers a transformative approach to addressing crime and conflict, shifting the focus from punishment to healing and reconciliation. The benefits of restorative justice extend beyond mere resolution of individual cases; they contribute to the personal growth of participants, the strengthening of community bonds, and the overall improvement of societal well-being. This chapter explores the numerous benefits of restorative justice, including increased empathy, reduced recidivism, and the fostering of community cohesion.

Increased Empathy

Empathy Development in Offenders

One of the most significant benefits of restorative justice is the development of empathy among offenders. Through restorative processes, offenders are given the opportunity to understand the impact of their actions on victims and the broader community.

- Understanding Harm: Hearing directly from victims about how the crime affected them can help offenders grasp the real-life consequences of their actions.

- Emotional Connection: By engaging in face-to-face dialogues with victims, offenders can develop an emotional connection and a deeper understanding of the pain they have caused.

Empathy in Victims and Community Members

Restorative justice also fosters empathy in victims and community members. The collaborative and inclusive nature of restorative processes encourages all participants to see the situation from multiple perspectives.

- Victims' Empathy: Victims, through the process, may come to understand the background and circumstances that led to the offender's actions, fostering a sense of empathy and compassion.

- Community Empathy: Community members who participate in or witness restorative justice processes often develop a greater empathy for both victims and offenders, understanding the broader social and psychological factors at play.

Reduced Recidivism

Accountability and Responsibility

Restorative justice holds offenders accountable in a constructive manner, encouraging them to take responsibility for their actions and to understand the harm they have caused. This accountability is a critical factor in reducing recidivism.

- Personal Responsibility: Offenders are more likely to change their behavior when they fully acknowledge the impact of their actions and feel a personal responsibility to make amends.

- Constructive Accountability: Unlike punitive systems that often alienate offenders, restorative justice seeks to reintegrate them into the community, fostering positive behavioral changes.

Support and Reintegration

Restorative justice processes often include plans for the offender's reintegration into society, providing support systems that help prevent reoffending.

- Support Networks: By involving community members and creating support networks, restorative justice helps offenders to find positive paths forward, reducing the likelihood of recidivism.

- Rehabilitation Programs: Many restorative justice agreements include participation in rehabilitation programs, further supporting the offender's personal development and reducing the risk of reoffending.

Fostering Community Cohesion

Strengthening Social Bonds

Restorative justice emphasizes the involvement of the community in the justice process, which strengthens social bonds and promotes community cohesion.

- Collective Involvement: By engaging the community in the resolution of conflicts, restorative justice fosters a sense of collective responsibility and solidarity.

- Building Trust: The process of coming together to address harm and seek resolution builds trust among community members, creating a more supportive and cohesive social fabric.

Community Healing

Restorative justice processes contribute to the healing of communities affected by crime, addressing not just the immediate harm but also the underlying issues that may have contributed to the conflict.

- Holistic Healing: By addressing the needs of victims, offenders, and the community, restorative justice promotes holistic healing and the restoration of social harmony.

- Preventing Future Conflicts: The collaborative approach helps to identify and address underlying issues, reducing the likelihood of future conflicts and fostering a safer, more resilient community.

Personal Growth and Transformation

Victims' Healing and Empowerment

For victims, restorative justice offers a pathway to healing and empowerment, helping them to regain a sense of control and agency.

- Voice and Validation: Victims have the opportunity to express their feelings and experiences, receiving validation and support from the community and the offender.

- Empowerment: By actively participating in the justice process, victims regain a sense of control over their lives, which is crucial for emotional and psychological recovery.

Offenders' Rehabilitation

Restorative justice provides offenders with the opportunity for personal growth and transformation, encouraging them to make positive changes in their lives.

- Self-Reflection: The process of acknowledging harm and engaging in dialogue with victims fosters self-reflection and personal accountability.

- Positive Identity Formation: Offenders are supported in developing a more positive self-identity, moving away from a criminal identity towards a constructive and community-oriented one.

Economic Benefits

Cost-Effectiveness

Restorative justice is often more cost-effective than traditional justice systems, which can have significant economic benefits for society.

- Reduced Incarceration Costs: By diverting offenders from incarceration and focusing on community-based resolutions, restorative justice can significantly reduce the costs associated with imprisonment.

- Efficiency: Restorative processes can be more efficient and quicker than traditional court proceedings, leading to faster resolutions and lower administrative costs.

Long-Term Economic Gains

The long-term economic benefits of restorative justice include the reduced social costs associated with recidivism and the enhanced productivity of rehabilitated offenders.

- Reduced Recidivism Costs: Lower recidivism rates translate into reduced costs for law enforcement, judicial proceedings, and incarceration.

- Productive Citizens: By supporting offenders in their rehabilitation and reintegration, restorative justice helps them to become productive members of society, contributing to the economy.

The benefits of restorative justice are far-reaching and multifaceted, encompassing increased empathy, reduced recidivism, and the fostering of community cohesion. By focusing on healing, accountability, and community involvement, restorative justice not only addresses the immediate harm caused by crime but also contributes to the long-term well-being of individuals and communities. Understanding these benefits is crucial for appreciating the transformative potential of restorative justice and advocating for its broader implementation in justice systems worldwide. As we continue to explore the various dimensions of restorative justice in this book, the insights gained from highlighting its benefits will serve as a foundation for understanding its broader implications and applications.

Address Challenges

While restorative justice offers numerous benefits, it also presents various challenges and risks that must be carefully managed to ensure its effectiveness and fairness. Understanding these challenges is essential for practitioners, policymakers, and communities to successfully implement and sustain restorative justice programs. This chapter identifies and analyzes the potential challenges associated with restorative justice and provides strategies to mitigate these issues.

Emotional and Psychological Challenges

Re-traumatization of Victims

Challenge: Victims may experience re-traumatization when recounting their experiences or facing the offender, potentially causing emotional distress and psychological harm.

Mitigation Strategies:

- Thorough Preparation: Prepare victims thoroughly before the restorative process, ensuring they understand what to expect and have strategies to cope with potential emotional triggers.

- Professional Support: Provide access to professional psychological support, such as counseling or therapy, to help victims process their emotions before, during, and after the restorative process.

- Voluntary Participation: Ensure that participation is entirely voluntary and that victims can withdraw at any time if they feel uncomfortable or distressed.

Emotional Vulnerability of Offenders

Challenge: Offenders may feel intense shame, guilt, or fear during the restorative process, which can be emotionally overwhelming and counterproductive.

Mitigation Strategies:

- Supportive Environment: Create a supportive and non-judgmental environment where offenders feel safe to express their emotions and take responsibility for their actions.

- Balanced Accountability: Emphasize accountability while providing emotional support to help offenders manage their feelings of shame and guilt constructively.

- Facilitator Training: Ensure facilitators are trained to handle emotional vulnerability and can provide appropriate support to offenders throughout the process.

Power Imbalances

Challenge: Power imbalances between victims and offenders, or among community members, can affect the fairness and effectiveness of the restorative process.

Mitigation Strategies:

- Skilled Facilitation: Utilize skilled facilitators who can recognize and address power imbalances, ensuring that all voices are heard and respected.

- Inclusive Practices: Develop inclusive practices that empower marginalized or less assertive participants, giving them equal opportunity to contribute to the process.

- Ongoing Monitoring: Continuously monitor the dynamics of the restorative process and make adjustments as needed to maintain balance and fairness.

Cultural Sensitivity and Diversity

Challenge: Restorative justice practices may not be equally applicable or effective across different cultural contexts, leading to misunderstandings or ineffective outcomes.

Mitigation Strategies:

- Cultural Competence: Develop cultural competence among facilitators and practitioners, ensuring they understand and respect the cultural backgrounds of participants.

- Tailored Approaches: Adapt restorative justice practices to fit the cultural context of the community, incorporating relevant cultural norms and traditions.

- Community Involvement: Engage community leaders and members in the design and implementation of restorative justice programs to ensure cultural appropriateness and acceptance.

Resistance and Skepticism

Challenge: Participants, communities, or stakeholders may resist or be skeptical of restorative justice practices, preferring traditional punitive approaches.

Mitigation Strategies:

- Education and Awareness: Provide education and awareness programs to inform stakeholders about the principles, benefits, and successes of restorative justice.

- Demonstrating Success: Highlight successful case studies and evidence-based outcomes to build confidence and support for restorative justice.

- Stakeholder Engagement: Actively engage stakeholders, including law enforcement, legal professionals, and community leaders, in the development and implementation of restorative justice programs.

Legal and Systemic Challenges

Challenge: Integrating restorative justice into existing legal and criminal justice systems can be complex and may encounter legal or procedural obstacles.

Mitigation Strategies:

- Policy Development: Advocate for policies and legislation that support the integration of restorative justice into the formal justice system.

- Collaborative Models: Develop collaborative models that combine restorative and retributive justice approaches, ensuring a seamless integration that respects legal frameworks.

- Training and Resources: Provide training and resources for legal professionals, law enforcement, and other stakeholders to facilitate the effective implementation of restorative justice within the existing system.

Consistency and Quality Control

Challenge: Ensuring consistency and quality in restorative justice practices can be challenging, especially as programs scale or are implemented in diverse contexts.

Mitigation Strategies:

- Standardized Protocols: Develop standardized protocols and guidelines for restorative justice practices to ensure consistency and quality.

- Ongoing Training: Provide ongoing training and professional development for facilitators and practitioners to maintain high standards of practice.

- Evaluation and Feedback: Implement regular evaluation and feedback mechanisms to monitor the effectiveness of restorative justice programs and make continuous improvements.

Funding and Sustainability

Challenge: Securing sufficient funding and resources to sustain restorative justice programs can be difficult, particularly in the long term.

Mitigation Strategies:

- Diverse Funding Sources: Seek funding from diverse sources, including government grants, private donations, and community fundraising efforts.

- Cost-Effectiveness: Highlight the cost-effectiveness of restorative justice compared to traditional punitive approaches to attract funding and support.

- Partnerships: Build partnerships with community organizations, educational institutions, and other stakeholders to share resources and ensure sustainability.

Addressing the challenges and risks associated with restorative justice is crucial for its successful implementation and sustainability. By identifying these challenges and employing strategies to mitigate them, practitioners and communities can create effective and fair restorative justice programs that maximize the benefits for all participants. As we continue to explore the various dimensions of restorative justice in this book, understanding and addressing these challenges will be essential for fostering a more compassionate and effective approach to justice.

Provide Practical Guidance

Implementing restorative justice effectively requires a comprehensive understanding of best practices and practical strategies. This chapter aims to offer detailed guidance on the implementation of restorative justice, including the necessary training for facilitators, key elements of successful programs, and case studies that illustrate best practices in action. By following these guidelines, practitioners can ensure that restorative justice processes are fair, effective, and transformative for all participants.

Best Practices for Implementing Restorative Justice

Establishing a Clear Framework

1. Define Objectives and Principles:

- Clearly articulate the objectives and principles of the restorative justice program. Ensure that all stakeholders understand and commit to these foundational elements.

- Objectives may include repairing harm, promoting healing, and reducing recidivism.

2. Develop Protocols and Procedures:

- Establish standardized protocols and procedures for conducting restorative justice processes. These should include guidelines for preparation, facilitation, and follow-up.

- Ensure that procedures are flexible enough to be adapted to individual cases while maintaining consistency and fairness.

3. Engage Stakeholders:

- Involve a broad range of stakeholders, including victims, offenders, community members, law enforcement, and legal professionals, in the design and implementation of the program.

- Build partnerships with community organizations, educational institutions, and other relevant entities to support the program.

Training for Facilitators

1. Comprehensive Training Programs:

- Develop and implement comprehensive training programs for facilitators, covering key aspects of restorative justice, such as active listening, conflict resolution, and trauma-informed practices.

- Training should include both theoretical knowledge and practical skills, with opportunities for role-playing and supervised practice.

2. Continuous Professional Development:

- Provide ongoing professional development opportunities for facilitators to ensure they remain current with best practices and emerging trends in restorative justice.

- Encourage facilitators to engage in peer support and mentoring, fostering a community of practice that promotes continuous learning and improvement.

3. Emotional Intelligence and Cultural Competence:

- Emphasize the importance of emotional intelligence and cultural competence in facilitator training. Facilitators must be able to navigate complex emotional dynamics and be sensitive to cultural differences.

- Provide specific training on recognizing and addressing power imbalances, ensuring that all participants feel respected and heard.

Implementing Restorative Justice Processes

1. Preparation:

- Conduct thorough preparation with all participants before the restorative justice process begins. This includes explaining the process, setting expectations, and providing emotional support.

- Ensure that participants are fully informed and willing to engage voluntarily.

2. Facilitation:

- Facilitate restorative justice meetings in a safe and supportive environment, where all participants feel comfortable expressing their emotions and perspectives.

- Use structured formats, such as circles or conferences, to guide the process and ensure that all voices are heard.

3. Follow-Up:

- Implement follow-up procedures to monitor the outcomes of the restorative justice process and provide ongoing support to participants.

- Assess the effectiveness of the agreements reached and make adjustments as necessary to ensure long-term success.

Case Studies Illustrating Best Practices

Case Study 1: Family Group Conferencing in New Zealand

Background:

- New Zealand has been a pioneer in incorporating restorative justice into its juvenile justice system through Family Group Conferencing (FGC).

Implementation:

- FGC involves the offender, victim, their families, and community representatives in a structured meeting to discuss the impact of the crime and agree on a plan for restitution.

- Facilitators are trained extensively in restorative justice principles, cultural competence, and conflict resolution.

Outcomes:

- The program has shown significant success in reducing recidivism rates among young offenders and promoting healing for victims.

- FGC has strengthened community bonds and provided a model for other countries to adapt and implement.

Case Study 2: Peacemaking Circles in Canada

Background:

- Peacemaking circles, rooted in Indigenous traditions, have been implemented in various communities across Canada to address both criminal and non-criminal conflicts.

Implementation:

- The circle process involves bringing together the victim, offender, community members, and a trained facilitator to engage in a respectful and open dialogue.

- Circles are guided by principles of equality, respect, and shared responsibility, with a focus on collective healing.

Outcomes:

- Peacemaking circles have been effective in addressing underlying issues, fostering empathy, and promoting long-term reconciliation.

- The process has been adapted for use in schools, workplaces, and other community settings, demonstrating its versatility and effectiveness.

Overcoming Common Challenges

1. Ensuring Voluntary Participation:

- Emphasize the voluntary nature of restorative justice to all participants, ensuring they understand their rights and are not coerced into participation.

- Provide alternative options for those who do not wish to participate in restorative processes.

2. Managing Emotional Intensity:

- Prepare participants for the emotional intensity of the process, offering strategies for managing strong emotions.

- Ensure that facilitators are equipped to provide emotional support and de-escalate conflicts as needed.

3. Addressing Power Imbalances:

- Train facilitators to recognize and address power imbalances, ensuring that all participants have an equal opportunity to speak and be heard.

- Implement practices that empower marginalized voices and promote fairness in the process.

Measuring Success and Making Improvements

1. Evaluating Outcomes:

- Develop robust evaluation methods to measure the success of restorative justice programs, including qualitative and quantitative assessments.

- Collect feedback from participants to understand their experiences and identify areas for improvement.

2. Continuous Improvement:

- Use evaluation results to make continuous improvements to the program, ensuring it remains responsive to the needs of participants and the community.

- Stay informed about emerging best practices and innovations in restorative justice, incorporating them into the program as appropriate.

Implementing restorative justice requires a thoughtful and well-planned approach, guided by best practices and informed by successful case studies. By providing comprehensive training for facilitators, establishing clear protocols, and engaging a broad range of stakeholders, practitioners can create effective and sustainable restorative justice programs. Addressing common challenges and continuously evaluating and improving the program will ensure that restorative justice can fulfill its promise of healing, accountability, and community cohesion. As we continue to explore the various dimensions of restorative justice in this book, the practical guidance provided in this chapter will serve as a foundation for successful implementation and positive outcomes.

Enhancing Effectiveness

Restorative justice has the potential to transform the way we address crime and conflict by focusing on healing and reconciliation rather than punishment. However, to maximize its effectiveness, it is crucial to understand the psychological and emotional impacts of restorative justice on all participants. By recognizing these impacts, programs can be tailored to enhance positive outcomes and address potential pitfalls, ensuring that restorative justice fulfills its promise of creating a more just and compassionate society.

Understanding Psychological and Emotional Impacts

Psychological Impacts

1. Empathy Development:

- For Offenders: Engaging directly with victims helps offenders understand the human impact of their actions, fostering empathy and remorse. This understanding is crucial for meaningful accountability and personal transformation.

- For Victims: Victims may develop empathy for offenders by hearing their stories and understanding the circumstances that led to the crime. This can facilitate forgiveness and emotional healing.

2. Reduction in Recidivism:

- Offenders who participate in restorative justice processes often exhibit lower rates of recidivism. Understanding the psychological mechanisms behind this, such as increased empathy and personal accountability, can help tailor programs to further reduce reoffending.

3. Emotional Healing:

- For Victims: Restorative justice provides a platform for victims to express their emotions and receive validation, which is essential for emotional healing and closure.

- For Offenders: Taking responsibility for their actions and making amends can alleviate feelings of guilt and shame, promoting psychological relief and rehabilitation.

Emotional Impacts

1. Empowerment:

- For Victims: Restorative justice empowers victims by giving them a voice in the justice process. This sense of control and participation is vital for their emotional recovery and empowerment.

- For Offenders: Offenders gain a sense of empowerment by taking responsibility and actively participating in their rehabilitation, which can foster a positive self-identity and personal growth.

2. Community Cohesion:

- Restorative justice fosters stronger community bonds by involving community members in the justice process. This collective participation promotes empathy, trust, and a sense of shared responsibility, enhancing community cohesion and resilience.

3. Emotional Risks:

- Re-traumatization: Victims may experience re-traumatization by recounting their experiences or facing the offender. Understanding this risk helps in providing adequate support and preparation to mitigate emotional distress.

- Emotional Overwhelm: Offenders may feel overwhelmed by shame, guilt, or fear during the process. Recognizing this allows facilitators to offer balanced support, ensuring constructive accountability without causing emotional harm.

Enhancing Effectiveness Through Tailored Programs

Individualized Support

1. Victim Support:

- Pre-Process Preparation: Prepare victims thoroughly before the restorative process, helping them understand what to expect and providing strategies to cope with potential emotional triggers.

- Ongoing Counseling: Offer ongoing psychological support through counseling or therapy to help victims process their emotions and navigate their healing journey.

2. Offender Support:

- Guided Self-Reflection: Facilitate guided self-reflection sessions where offenders can explore the impact of their actions and develop a deeper understanding of their behavior.

- Reintegration Programs: Develop comprehensive reintegration programs that provide education, vocational training, and community service opportunities to support offenders in building a positive future.

Facilitator Training

1. Emotional Intelligence:

- Train facilitators in emotional intelligence to navigate complex emotional dynamics effectively. This includes active listening, empathy, and conflict resolution skills.

- Ensure facilitators can recognize and address emotional vulnerabilities, providing the necessary support to participants throughout the process.

2. Trauma-Informed Practices:

- Incorporate trauma-informed practices into facilitator training, ensuring they understand the effects of trauma on behavior and can create a safe, supportive environment for participants.

- Provide strategies for facilitators to help participants manage strong emotions and avoid re-traumatization.

Program Design

1. Flexible Frameworks:

- Design flexible frameworks that can be adapted to individual cases while maintaining core restorative principles. This allows for a personalized approach that meets the unique needs of each participant.

- Ensure protocols and procedures are clearly defined yet adaptable, enabling facilitators to respond to the specific dynamics of each case.

2. Community Involvement:

- Engage community members in the design and implementation of restorative justice programs to ensure cultural relevance and community buy-in.

- Promote community education and awareness to build support for restorative justice and encourage active participation.

Evaluating and Improving Restorative Justice Programs

Continuous Feedback

1. Participant Feedback:

- Collect feedback from all participants—victims, offenders, and community members—to understand their experiences and identify areas for improvement.

- Use surveys, interviews, and focus groups to gather comprehensive feedback and ensure diverse perspectives are represented.

2. Facilitator Insights:

- Encourage facilitators to provide regular feedback on the process, challenges encountered, and suggestions for improvement.

- Create a supportive environment where facilitators can share their experiences and learn from each other.

Data-Driven Improvements

1. Quantitative Measures:

- Implement quantitative measures to evaluate the effectiveness of restorative justice programs, such as recidivism rates, participant satisfaction, and community impact.

- Use data analytics to identify trends, measure success, and pinpoint areas needing adjustment.

2. Qualitative Analysis:

- Conduct qualitative analysis of participant narratives, case studies, and facilitator reports to gain deeper insights into the emotional and psychological impacts of restorative justice.

- Use qualitative data to complement quantitative findings, providing a holistic understanding of program effectiveness.

Case Studies: Learning from Successes

Case Study 1: Youth Offender Program

Background:

- A restorative justice program for youth offenders was implemented in a mid-sized city to address juvenile delinquency.

Implementation:

- The program involved victim-offender mediation, community service, and mentorship.

- Facilitators received specialized training in youth development and trauma-informed practices.

Outcomes:

- Recidivism rates among participants dropped significantly compared to those in traditional juvenile justice systems.

- Participants reported increased empathy, accountability, and positive behavior changes.

Lessons Learned:

- Tailored support for youth offenders, including mentorship and community involvement, is crucial for effective rehabilitation.

- Trauma-informed practices enhance the emotional safety and effectiveness of restorative justice processes.

Case Study 2: Domestic Violence Restorative Program

Background:

- A restorative justice program was introduced to address domestic violence cases in a suburban community.

Implementation:

- The program included victim-offender dialogues, therapy sessions, and community support groups.

- Facilitators were trained in domestic violence dynamics and emotional intelligence.

Outcomes:

- Victims reported a sense of empowerment and emotional healing, while offenders showed increased accountability and reduced reoffending rates.

- Community support groups strengthened social bonds and provided ongoing support for both victims and offenders.

Lessons Learned:

- Specialized training for facilitators in domestic violence is essential for handling sensitive cases.

- Community support plays a vital role in the long-term success of restorative justice programs.

Understanding the psychological and emotional impacts of restorative justice is essential for enhancing its effectiveness. By recognizing these impacts, programs can be tailored to maximize positive outcomes and address potential pitfalls. Individualized support for victims and offenders, comprehensive training for facilitators, and flexible program design are critical components of successful restorative justice implementation. Continuous evaluation and learning from successful case studies ensure that restorative justice programs can evolve and improve, ultimately creating a more just and compassionate society. As we continue to explore restorative justice in this book, the insights gained from enhancing effectiveness will serve as a foundation for understanding its broader implications and applications.

Supporting Participants

One of the critical aspects of restorative justice is the comprehensive support provided to all participants—victims, offenders, and community members. Understanding the psychological and emotional impacts of restorative justice enables practitioners to offer better support, ensuring that the needs of all participants are met throughout the process. This chapter explores strategies for effectively supporting participants, highlighting the importance of preparation, ongoing support, and tailored interventions.

Supporting Victims

Preparation and Pre-Process Support

1. Thorough Preparation:

   - Information and Clarity: Provide detailed information about the restorative justice process, including what to expect, the roles of various participants, and potential outcomes. This helps to reduce anxiety and uncertainty.

   - Emotional Readiness: Assess the emotional readiness of victims to participate in the process. Ensure they understand that their participation is voluntary and that they can opt out at any time.

2. Building Trust and Safety:

   - Safe Environment: Create a safe and supportive environment where victims feel comfortable expressing their emotions and sharing their experiences.

   - Confidentiality: Emphasize the importance of confidentiality in the process to protect victims' privacy and build trust.

During the Process

1. Active Listening and Validation:

- Empathetic Listening: Facilitators should practice active listening, validating victims' feelings and experiences. This helps victims feel heard and respected.

- Emotional Support: Provide immediate emotional support during the process, such as having a counselor available if needed.

2. Empowerment and Agency:

- Voice and Participation: Ensure that victims have a central role in the process, allowing them to express their needs, ask questions, and influence the outcomes.

- Restorative Agreements: Involve victims in crafting restorative agreements, ensuring that their needs for reparation and closure are addressed.

Post-Process Support

1. Follow-Up:

- Regular Check-Ins: Conduct regular follow-ups with victims to assess their well-being and provide ongoing support. This can include phone calls, meetings, or counseling sessions.

- Long-Term Support: Offer long-term support options, such as therapy or support groups, to help victims continue their healing journey.

2. Feedback and Improvement:

- Collect Feedback: Gather feedback from victims about their experience with the restorative justice process. Use this feedback to improve the program and address any identified issues.

- Continuous Improvement: Continuously improve support mechanisms based on victims' feedback and evolving best practices in restorative justice.

Supporting Offenders

Preparation and Pre-Process Support

1. Initial Assessment:

- Readiness and Willingness: Assess offenders' readiness and willingness to participate in restorative justice. Ensure they understand the purpose and expectations of the process.

- Support Needs: Identify any specific support needs, such as mental health issues, substance abuse, or educational needs, and provide appropriate resources.

2. Building Trust and Accountability:

- Transparent Communication: Communicate transparently about the process, addressing any concerns or misconceptions offenders may have.

- Encouraging Accountability: Emphasize the importance of accountability and personal responsibility in a supportive manner.

During the Process

1. Facilitated Dialogue:

- Guided Reflection: Facilitate guided reflection sessions where offenders can explore the impact of their actions and develop empathy for the victims.

- Respectful Interaction: Ensure that interactions between offenders and victims are respectful and constructive, promoting genuine understanding and remorse.

2. Supportive Environment:

- Emotional Support: Provide emotional support during the process, helping offenders manage feelings of shame, guilt, or fear.

- Balanced Approach: Balance accountability with support, ensuring that offenders feel encouraged to make amends without feeling overwhelmed by their emotions.

Post-Process Support

1. Reintegration Programs:

- Educational and Vocational Support: Offer educational and vocational training programs to help offenders build skills and secure employment, facilitating their reintegration into society.

- Community Service: Incorporate community service opportunities that allow offenders to give back to the community and build positive relationships.

2. Ongoing Counseling:

- Mental Health Support: Provide ongoing mental health support, such as counseling or therapy, to help offenders address underlying issues and continue their personal growth.

- Mentorship Programs: Establish mentorship programs where offenders can receive guidance and support from positive role models.

Supporting Community Members

Preparation and Pre-Process Support

1. Community Engagement:

- Awareness Programs: Conduct awareness programs to educate community members about restorative justice and its benefits, building community support and involvement.

- Involvement Opportunities: Create opportunities for community members to get involved in the restorative justice process, such as volunteering or participating in community circles.

2. Building Trust and Inclusivity:

- Inclusive Practices: Ensure that the restorative justice process is inclusive, allowing diverse community voices to be heard and respected.

- Transparency: Maintain transparency about the process and its goals, fostering trust and confidence among community members.

During the Process

1. Active Participation:

- Empowering Voices: Empower community members to actively participate in the process, sharing their perspectives and contributing to the resolution.

- Collective Responsibility: Promote a sense of collective responsibility for addressing harm and supporting healing within the community.

2. Support and Empathy:

- Building Empathy: Facilitate dialogues that build empathy among community members, helping them understand the experiences of victims and offenders.

- Emotional Support: Provide emotional support to community members who may be affected by the process, such as those experiencing secondary trauma.

Post-Process Support

1. Community Healing:

- Support Groups: Establish support groups for community members to continue the dialogue and healing process, fostering ongoing empathy and understanding.

- Community Projects: Initiate community projects that address underlying issues contributing to crime and conflict, promoting long-term community resilience.

2. Feedback and Improvement:

- Collect Feedback: Gather feedback from community members about their experience with the restorative justice process, using it to improve and adapt the program.

- Continuous Engagement: Maintain continuous engagement with the community, ensuring that restorative justice remains a collaborative and evolving effort.

Supporting participants throughout the restorative justice process is essential for maximizing its effectiveness and ensuring positive outcomes for all involved. By providing comprehensive support to victims, offenders, and community members, practitioners can address the psychological and emotional impacts of restorative justice, fostering healing, accountability, and community cohesion. Understanding the unique needs of each participant group and tailoring support accordingly is crucial for the success of restorative justice programs. As we continue to explore restorative justice in this book, the insights gained from supporting participants will serve as a foundation for understanding its broader implications and applications.

Promoting Widespread Adoption

Restorative justice offers a transformative approach to dealing with crime and conflict, emphasizing healing and reconciliation over punishment. For restorative justice to reach its full potential, it must be adopted more broadly within justice systems and communities worldwide. This chapter explores strategies for promoting widespread adoption, including demonstrating benefits, addressing challenges, and engaging key stakeholders.

Demonstrating the Benefits

Evidence-Based Outcomes

1. Reduced Recidivism:

- Research Findings: Numerous studies have shown that restorative justice significantly reduces recidivism rates compared to traditional punitive approaches. Highlighting these findings can convince policymakers and justice professionals of its effectiveness.

- Case Studies: Presenting successful case studies, such as reduced reoffending rates among participants, can provide concrete examples of the benefits.

2. Victim Satisfaction:

- Positive Feedback: Victims who participate in restorative justice processes often report higher satisfaction levels due to the opportunity to express their feelings and receive restitution.

- Empowerment and Healing: Emphasize how restorative justice empowers victims, promotes healing, and provides a sense of closure that traditional systems often fail to deliver.

3. Community Cohesion:

- Strengthening Bonds: Restorative justice fosters stronger community ties by involving community members in the justice process, promoting empathy and collective responsibility.

- Long-Term Safety: Communities that adopt restorative practices often experience long-term safety and stability, as underlying issues are addressed collaboratively.

Economic Benefits

1. Cost-Effectiveness:

- Lower Costs: Restorative justice processes typically cost less than incarceration and lengthy court proceedings. Highlighting these economic benefits can appeal to policymakers focused on budgetary constraints.

- Efficient Resolution: The efficiency of restorative justice processes can reduce the burden on the judicial system, freeing up resources for other needs.

2. Economic Productivity:

- Reintegration: Successful reintegration of offenders into society as productive members can lead to economic benefits, such as increased employment and reduced social welfare dependency.

Addressing Challenges

Overcoming Resistance and Skepticism

1. Education and Awareness:

- Public Campaigns: Implement public awareness campaigns to educate the community about restorative justice, its principles, and its benefits. Use media, social networks, and public forums to disseminate information.

- Workshops and Seminars: Conduct workshops and seminars for legal professionals, law enforcement, and community leaders to address misconceptions and provide evidence-based knowledge about restorative justice.

2. Building Trust:

- Transparent Practices: Ensure that restorative justice practices are transparent and inclusive, building trust among participants and stakeholders.

- Success Stories: Share success stories and testimonials from participants who have benefited from restorative justice, reinforcing its positive impact.

Ensuring Quality and Consistency

1. Standardized Training:

- Comprehensive Training Programs: Develop standardized training programs for facilitators to ensure they possess the necessary skills and knowledge to conduct restorative justice processes effectively.

- Certification: Implement certification processes for facilitators to maintain high standards of practice and accountability.

2. Monitoring and Evaluation:

- Regular Assessments: Conduct regular assessments of restorative justice programs to evaluate their effectiveness and identify areas for improvement.

- Feedback Mechanisms: Establish feedback mechanisms for participants to share their experiences and suggestions for enhancing the process.

Integrating with Traditional Justice Systems

1. Policy Development:

- Legislative Support: Advocate for policies and legislation that support the integration of restorative justice into the traditional justice system, providing a legal framework for its application.

- Collaborative Models: Develop collaborative models that combine restorative and retributive justice approaches, ensuring a seamless integration that respects legal standards.

2. Stakeholder Engagement:

- Partnerships: Build partnerships with key stakeholders, including judges, prosecutors, defense attorneys, and law enforcement, to promote restorative justice as a complementary approach.

- Pilot Programs: Implement pilot programs within the existing justice system to demonstrate the effectiveness of restorative justice and build support for broader adoption.

Engaging Key Stakeholders

Community Involvement

1. Grassroots Movements:

- Community Initiatives: Encourage grassroots movements to advocate for restorative justice within their communities, fostering local ownership and engagement.

- Volunteer Opportunities: Create opportunities for community members to volunteer in restorative justice programs, enhancing their understanding and commitment to the process.

2. Local Leaders:

- Engage Leaders: Involve local leaders, such as religious leaders, educators, and civic organizers, in promoting restorative justice and building community support.

- Public Endorsements: Seek public endorsements from respected community figures to lend credibility and visibility to restorative justice initiatives.

Educational Institutions

1. Curriculum Integration:

- Educational Programs: Integrate restorative justice principles into school curricula, teaching students about conflict resolution, empathy, and accountability from a young age.

- School-Based Programs: Implement restorative justice programs in schools to address disciplinary issues, promote a positive school climate, and reduce bullying.

2. Research and Development:

- Academic Research: Encourage academic institutions to conduct research on restorative justice, contributing to the evidence base and exploring innovative practices.

- Collaborative Projects: Partner with universities and research centers to develop and evaluate restorative justice programs, ensuring continuous improvement and adaptation.

Government and Legal Systems

1. Advocacy and Lobbying:

- Policy Advocacy: Engage in advocacy efforts to influence policymakers and legislators to support restorative justice initiatives through policy changes and funding.

- Legal Reforms: Lobby for legal reforms that facilitate the integration of restorative justice into the criminal justice system, ensuring its legitimacy and effectiveness.

2. Interagency Collaboration:

- Cross-Agency Teams: Form cross-agency teams that include representatives from the judiciary, law enforcement, social services, and restorative justice organizations to coordinate efforts and share best practices.

- Shared Resources: Promote the sharing of resources, data, and expertise among agencies to enhance the implementation and impact of restorative justice programs.

Promoting the widespread adoption of restorative justice requires a multifaceted approach that demonstrates its benefits, addresses challenges, and engages key stakeholders. By educating the public, ensuring quality and consistency, integrating restorative practices with traditional justice systems, and fostering community involvement, restorative justice can become a mainstream approach to addressing crime and conflict. As we continue to explore restorative justice in this book, the insights gained from promoting widespread adoption will serve as a foundation for understanding its broader implications and applications, ultimately contributing to a more just and compassionate society.

CHAPTER 02

UNDERSTANDING RESTORATIVE JUSTICE

Definition and Principles

Restorative justice represents a fundamental shift in how societies address crime and conflict. Rather than focusing solely on punishment, restorative justice emphasizes healing, accountability, and reparation, involving all stakeholders in a collaborative process. This chapter delves into the definition and key principles of restorative justice, highlighting its transformative potential and practical applications.

Definition of Restorative Justice

Restorative justice is a philosophy and practice designed to repair the harm caused by criminal behavior through inclusive and participatory processes. It contrasts with traditional retributive justice systems, which prioritize punishment and deterrence. Instead, restorative justice seeks to restore relationships, mend the social fabric, and promote long-term community well-being. The core components of restorative justice include:

- Healing: Addressing the emotional, psychological, and material needs of victims, offenders, and the community.

- Accountability: Encouraging offenders to take responsibility for their actions and understand the impact of their behavior.

- Reparation: Developing mutually agreed-upon plans to make amends for the harm caused and prevent future offenses.

Key Principles of Restorative Justice

Repairing Harm

Emphasizing Healing:

- Victims' Needs: Restorative justice places victims at the center of the process, recognizing their need for healing, validation, and reparation. This focus on victims' needs ensures that they receive the support and closure necessary to move forward.

- Offenders' Responsibility: Offenders are encouraged to understand the consequences of their actions and to actively participate in repairing the harm they have caused.

This responsibility is crucial for their personal growth and rehabilitation.

Holistic Approach:

- Emotional and Psychological Healing: Restorative justice acknowledges the emotional and psychological harm caused by crime, providing a space for victims and offenders to express their feelings and experiences. This holistic approach promotes deeper healing and reconciliation.

- Material Reparation: In addition to emotional healing, restorative justice often includes material reparation, such as financial compensation or community service, to address the tangible impacts of the crime.

Inclusive Decision-Making

Involving All Stakeholders:

- Victims: Victims are given a voice in the justice process, allowing them to share their stories, express their needs, and participate in decision-making. This inclusion fosters a sense of empowerment and validation.

- Offenders: Offenders are actively involved in the process, taking responsibility for their actions and working towards making amends. This participation is essential for their rehabilitation and reintegration.

- Community Members: Community members play a crucial role in restorative justice, supporting both victims and offenders and helping to develop and implement reparation plans. Their involvement strengthens community bonds and promotes collective healing.

Collaborative Processes:

- Dialogue and Mediation: Restorative justice processes often involve facilitated dialogues or mediations, where all stakeholders come together to discuss the impact of the crime and develop a plan for reparation. These collaborative processes encourage mutual understanding and empathy.

- Consensus-Based Decisions: Decisions in restorative justice are typically reached through consensus, ensuring that all voices are heard and respected. This approach fosters a sense of shared responsibility and commitment to the outcomes.

Reintegration

Supporting Offenders:

- Dignity and Respect: Restorative justice seeks to reintegrate offenders into society with dignity and respect, recognizing their potential for change and growth. This support is essential for preventing recidivism and promoting long-term rehabilitation.

- Tailored Reentry Plans: Offenders often receive tailored reentry plans that address their specific needs, such as education, employment, and mental health support. These plans help them build a positive future and avoid reoffending.

Community Involvement:

- Building Support Networks: Restorative justice emphasizes the importance of community support for reintegration. Community members, mentors, and support groups can provide the necessary guidance and encouragement for offenders to succeed.

- Restorative Circles: Reintegration circles or community circles can be used to support offenders as they reenter society. These circles provide a platform for ongoing dialogue, accountability, and mutual support.

Practical Applications of Restorative Justice Principles

Victim-Offender Mediation

Process:

- Victim-offender mediation involves direct dialogue between the victim and the offender, facilitated by a trained mediator. The process allows both parties to express their feelings, discuss the impact of the crime, and develop a plan for reparation.

Benefits:

- Empathy and Understanding: Mediation fosters empathy and understanding between victims and offenders, promoting healing and accountability.

- Tailored Reparation: The reparation plan developed during mediation is tailored to the specific needs and circumstances of the victim and offender, ensuring that it is meaningful and effective.

Family Group Conferencing

Process:

- Family group conferencing brings together the victim, offender, their families, and other supporters in a structured meeting. The group collaboratively develops a plan to address the harm caused and support the offender's reintegration.

Benefits:

- Supportive Environment: The involvement of family and supporters creates a supportive environment for both the victim and the offender, enhancing the effectiveness of the process.

- Holistic Solutions: Family group conferencing often results in holistic solutions that address the emotional, psychological, and material needs of all parties involved.

Community Restorative Circles

Process:

- Community restorative circles involve a broader group of community members in the restorative process.

Participants sit in a circle and use a talking piece to ensure respectful and egalitarian dialogue.

Benefits:

- Community Engagement: Community circles engage a wide range of stakeholders, fostering community cohesion and collective responsibility.

- Shared Healing: The process promotes shared healing and mutual support, strengthening the social fabric of the community.

Restorative justice, with its focus on repairing harm, inclusive decision-making, and reintegration, offers a powerful alternative to traditional retributive justice systems. By involving all stakeholders in a collaborative process that emphasizes healing and accountability, restorative justice can transform the way societies address crime and conflict. Understanding and applying the key principles of restorative justice—repairing harm, inclusive decision-making, and reintegration—are essential for creating effective and compassionate justice systems that promote long-term community well-being. As we continue to explore restorative justice in this book, these principles will serve as a foundation for understanding its broader implications and applications.

Historical Context and Evolution

Restorative justice, while gaining prominence in modern justice systems, has deep historical roots and a rich evolution. Understanding its historical context and evolution is crucial to appreciating its contemporary application and the underlying philosophies that drive its principles. This chapter traces the origins of restorative justice from indigenous practices to its modern resurgence, highlighting key milestones and developments along the way.

Indigenous Practices

Indigenous North American Traditions

Among Native American tribes, justice was traditionally viewed as a communal responsibility. Practices focused on restoring harmony and addressing the needs of all affected parties. Key elements included:

- Peacemaking Circles: Community members would gather in circles to discuss conflicts and collectively decide on resolutions. This practice emphasized dialogue, mutual respect, and collective healing.

- Shaming and Reconciliation: Offenders were encouraged to take responsibility for their actions and to make amends with those they harmed. The community played a crucial role in supporting both the victim and the offender.

African Traditions

In many African cultures, restorative justice principles were embedded in communal life:

- Ubuntu Philosophy: The concept of Ubuntu emphasizes human interconnectedness and community harmony. Justice practices under Ubuntu focused on restoring relationships and reintegrating offenders into the community.

- Gacaca Courts in Rwanda: These traditional community courts were used to address conflicts and crimes, including after the Rwandan genocide. The focus was on truth-telling, accountability, and reconciliation.

Maori Traditions in New Zealand

The Maori people have long practiced forms of restorative justice:

- Whanau Conferencing: This approach involves extended family members in resolving conflicts and supporting both victims and offenders. The principles of collective responsibility and restoring balance are central to this practice.

Early Modern Influences

Quaker Contributions

In the 17th century, the Quakers introduced restorative principles into their justice practices in England and North America:

- Inner Light and Forgiveness: Quaker beliefs in the inner light within each person and the power of forgiveness influenced their approach to justice. They emphasized reconciliation and rehabilitation over punishment.

- Penitentiary Reform: Quaker efforts led to the establishment of penitentiaries aimed at providing a space for reflection and repentance, rather than mere incarceration.

19th and 20th Century Reform Movements

Various reform movements during the 19th and 20th centuries laid the groundwork for modern restorative justice:

- Juvenile Justice Reform: Reformers emphasized rehabilitation over punishment for young offenders, advocating for systems that addressed their social and psychological needs.

- Victims' Rights Movement: In the latter half of the 20th century, the victims' rights movement highlighted the need for justice systems to address the needs and rights of victims, paving the way for restorative practices.

Modern Resurgence

The 1970s and 1980s: A Turning Point

The modern restorative justice movement gained significant momentum during the 1970s and 1980s:

- Victim-Offender Reconciliation Program (VORP): In 1974, the first formal VORP was established in Kitchener, Ontario, Canada. This program facilitated direct dialogues between victims and offenders, focusing on healing and reparation.

- Expansion of Restorative Practices: The success of early VORP programs inspired the development of various restorative practices, including family group conferencing and community restorative circles.

International Adoption and Adaptation

Restorative justice principles began to be incorporated into national and international justice systems during the late 20th and early 21st centuries:

- New Zealand: In 1989, New Zealand implemented family group conferencing as part of its juvenile justice system, influenced by Maori traditions. This model has since been adopted and adapted in various countries.

- United Kingdom: The UK integrated restorative justice into its criminal justice system, particularly in youth justice, emphasizing community involvement and reparation.

- United Nations: In 2002, the UN adopted the Basic Principles on the Use of Restorative Justice Programmes in Criminal Matters, encouraging member states to integrate restorative practices into their justice systems.

Key Historical Milestones

Development of Family Group Conferencing

Origin:

- Family group conferencing (FGC) was developed in New Zealand, inspired by Maori traditions. It involves victims, offenders, their families, and community members in resolving conflicts and deciding on reparation.

Impact:

- FGC has been credited with reducing recidivism and improving outcomes for young offenders. It has been adopted in various countries and contexts, demonstrating the adaptability and effectiveness of restorative justice.

Revival of Gacaca Courts in Rwanda

Context:

- After the 1994 genocide, Rwanda faced the challenge of achieving justice and reconciliation for the massive number of crimes committed.

Implementation:

- Rwanda revived the traditional Gacaca courts to handle genocide cases, focusing on truth-telling, accountability, and community healing.

Outcomes:

- The Gacaca courts facilitated a significant number of cases, contributing to the nation's recovery and highlighting the potential of restorative justice in post-conflict settings.

Introduction of Restorative Practices in Schools

Development:

- Restorative practices began to be implemented in educational settings to address conflict, reduce disciplinary issues, and promote positive school climates.

Benefits:

- Schools that adopted restorative practices reported reduced bullying, improved student behavior, and enhanced relationships among students and staff.

Evolution in the 21st Century

Integration with Traditional Justice Systems

Hybrid Models:

- The 21st century has seen efforts to integrate restorative justice with traditional justice systems. Hybrid models combine restorative and retributive approaches, providing a more holistic and effective justice process.

Collaborative Efforts:

- Collaborative efforts between restorative justice practitioners and traditional justice professionals have led to the development of integrated frameworks that respect legal standards while promoting healing and reconciliation.

Expanding Applications

Beyond Criminal Justice:

- Restorative justice principles have been applied in various contexts beyond criminal justice, including schools, workplaces, and communities. This broader application demonstrates the versatility and effectiveness of restorative practices.

Innovation and Research:

- Ongoing research and innovation in restorative justice continue to refine practices, measure outcomes, and address challenges. Academic institutions, non-profit organizations, and governmental bodies collaborate to advance the field.

The historical context and evolution of restorative justice reveal a rich tapestry of traditions, influences, and innovations that have shaped its development. From indigenous practices to modern applications, restorative justice has consistently emphasized the importance of healing, accountability, and community involvement. Understanding this history is crucial for appreciating the depth and potential of restorative justice as a transformative approach to addressing crime and conflict. As we continue to explore restorative justice in this book, the insights gained from its historical context and evolution will provide a solid foundation for understanding its broader implications and applications.

CHAPTER 03

PSYCHOLOGY FOUNDATIONS OF RESTORATIVE JUSTICE

Retributive Justice

Introduction

Retributive justice is a concept that has dominated criminal justice systems for centuries. Rooted in the belief that punishment is a necessary response to wrongdoing, retributive justice seeks to balance the scales by ensuring that offenders receive their just deserts. This chapter delves into the principles, historical evolution, psychological underpinnings, and criticisms of retributive justice, providing a comprehensive understanding of its role and limitations in contemporary justice systems.

Principles of Retributive Justice

Just Deserts

The core principle of retributive justice is that offenders deserve to be punished in proportion to the severity of their crimes. This concept of "just deserts" asserts that punishment should be neither excessively harsh nor unduly lenient but should correspond to the moral gravity of the offense.

- Proportionality: The punishment must fit the crime, ensuring a fair and balanced response to wrongdoing.

- Moral Order: Retributive justice is based on the idea that a moral order exists, and any violation of this order must be addressed through punishment to restore balance.

Accountability and Responsibility

Retributive justice emphasizes the importance of holding offenders accountable for their actions. By imposing punishment, society reinforces the notion that individuals are responsible for their behavior and must face the consequences of their choices.

- Moral Responsibility: Offenders are seen as moral agents who have freely chosen to commit a crime and, therefore, must be held accountable.

- Deterrence: Punishment serves as a deterrent to both the individual offender and others who might contemplate similar actions, reinforcing societal norms and discouraging criminal behavior.

Historical Evolution of Retributive Justice

Ancient Foundations

Retributive justice has ancient roots, with early legal codes emphasizing punishment as a means of maintaining social order. Notable examples include:

- Code of Hammurabi: One of the oldest known legal codes, the Code of Hammurabi (circa 1754 BCE) enshrined the principle of "an eye for an eye," emphasizing proportional punishment.

- Roman Law: Roman legal traditions also emphasized retribution, with punishments designed to fit the severity of the offense and maintain public order.

Medieval and Enlightenment Influences

During the medieval period, retributive justice continued to play a central role in legal systems, often intertwined with religious concepts of sin and divine retribution. The Enlightenment era brought significant philosophical contributions to the concept of retributive justice:

- Immanuel Kant: The philosopher Immanuel Kant articulated a formal theory of retributive justice, arguing that punishment is a moral imperative and a categorical duty of the state. According to Kant, punishment respects the autonomy and dignity of individuals by treating them as rational agents accountable for their actions.

- G.W.F. Hegel: Hegel expanded on retributive principles, viewing punishment as a necessary response to crime to restore the moral order and reaffirm the rights of victims.

Psychological Underpinnings of Retributive Justice

Moral Outrage and Retribution

Psychologically, retributive justice taps into innate human responses to wrongdoing, including moral outrage and a desire for retribution. These emotional reactions play a crucial role in shaping societal attitudes towards punishment:

- Moral Emotions: Feelings of anger, disgust, and moral indignation often accompany perceptions of injustice, driving a collective desire to see offenders punished.

- Restoration of Moral Balance: Punishment is seen as a way to restore moral balance and affirm societal values, providing psychological closure to victims and the community.

Cognitive Dissonance

Retributive justice also addresses cognitive dissonance, a psychological phenomenon where individuals experience discomfort when their beliefs and actions are in conflict. By punishing offenders, society resolves this dissonance, reinforcing the belief that justice prevails and that moral transgressions have consequences.

- Consistency in Beliefs: Punishment aligns societal actions with moral beliefs, reducing cognitive dissonance and reinforcing the legitimacy of the justice system.

- Social Cohesion: By addressing wrongdoing through punishment, retributive justice helps maintain social cohesion and trust in legal institutions.

Criticisms of Retributive Justice

Ineffectiveness in Rehabilitation

One of the primary criticisms of retributive justice is its limited effectiveness in rehabilitating offenders. Punishment alone does not address the underlying causes of criminal behavior or support offenders in making positive changes.

- Lack of Rehabilitation: Retributive justice often neglects the need for rehabilitative measures, such as education, therapy, and vocational training, which are essential for reducing recidivism and promoting reintegration.

- Cycle of Crime: Without addressing the root causes of crime, retributive justice can perpetuate a cycle of offending, with individuals returning to criminal behavior after serving their punishment.

Disproportionality and Inequity

Critics argue that retributive justice can result in disproportionate and inequitable outcomes, with marginalized groups often receiving harsher punishments than their more privileged counterparts.

- Bias and Discrimination: Implicit biases and systemic discrimination within the justice system can lead to unequal application of retributive principles, undermining fairness and justice.

- Over-Punishment: In some cases, retributive justice can lead to excessively harsh punishments that do not fit the crime, violating the principle of proportionality and causing undue harm.

Psychological Harm

The focus on punishment in retributive justice can cause psychological harm to both offenders and victims:

- Offenders: Harsh punishments can lead to feelings of resentment, shame, and hopelessness, hindering rehabilitation and increasing the risk of reoffending.

- Victims: While some victims may find solace in seeing offenders punished, others may experience prolonged distress and a lack of closure if the justice process does not address their emotional and psychological needs.

Retributive justice, with its emphasis on punishment and accountability, has played a central role in legal systems for centuries. While it taps into deep-seated human emotions and provides a clear framework for addressing wrongdoing, it also has significant limitations and criticisms. Understanding the principles, historical evolution, and psychological underpinnings of retributive justice is essential for appreciating its role in contemporary justice systems and exploring alternatives that address its shortcomings. As we continue to explore the psychological foundations of restorative justice in this book, the insights gained from examining retributive justice will provide a valuable context for understanding the transformative potential of restorative approaches.

Distributive Justice: Fair Allocation of Resources and Opportunities

Introduction

Distributive justice is concerned with the fair allocation of resources and opportunities within a society. It addresses the moral and ethical questions surrounding how goods, wealth, and opportunities should be distributed among individuals and groups. This chapter delves into the principles, theories, and psychological foundations of distributive justice, exploring its implications for social equity and the overall well-being of society.

Principles of Distributive Justice

Fairness and Equality

At the heart of distributive justice is the principle of fairness. This principle asserts that resources and opportunities should be distributed in a manner that is fair and just to all members of society. Key aspects include:

- Equality of Opportunity: Ensuring that all individuals have equal access to opportunities, such as education, employment, and healthcare.

- Equity: Adjusting distributions to account for differences in individuals' circumstances and needs, aiming for a more equitable outcome.

Merit and Desert

Another principle of distributive justice is that rewards should be allocated based on merit and desert. This perspective holds that individuals should receive benefits commensurate with their contributions or efforts.

- Merit-Based Distribution: Allocating resources based on individuals' talents, efforts, and achievements.

- Desert-Based Distribution: Ensuring that individuals who contribute more to society or exhibit greater effort receive proportionally greater rewards.

Need and Welfare

The principle of need focuses on distributing resources to meet individuals' basic needs and promote their welfare. This approach emphasizes:

- Meeting Basic Needs: Ensuring that all members of society have access to essential resources such as food, shelter, healthcare, and education.

- Promoting Well-Being: Allocating resources in a way that enhances the overall well-being and quality of life for everyone, particularly the most vulnerable members of society.

Theories of Distributive Justice

Utilitarianism

Utilitarianism is a consequentialist theory that suggests resources should be distributed to maximize overall happiness or utility. Key aspects include:

- Greatest Good for the Greatest Number: Resources should be allocated in a way that produces the greatest net benefit for society as a whole.

- Cost-Benefit Analysis: Decisions about distribution should involve weighing the costs and benefits to ensure the most efficient allocation of resources.

Egalitarianism

Egalitarianism advocates for equal distribution of resources and opportunities, arguing that inequality is inherently unjust. Key components include:

- Strict Equality: Ensuring that all individuals receive the same share of resources and opportunities, regardless of their circumstances or contributions.

- Redistribution: Implementing policies and practices that redistribute wealth and resources to reduce inequalities and promote social justice.

John Rawls' Theory of Justice

Philosopher John Rawls proposed a theory of justice based on the principles of fairness and equality. Key elements include:

- Original Position and Veil of Ignorance: Rawls' thought experiment where individuals design a just society from an original position of equality, behind a veil of ignorance that prevents them from knowing their own social status.

- Principles of Justice: Rawls formulated two key principles:

- Equal Basic Liberties: Each person should have an equal right to the most extensive basic liberties compatible with similar liberties for others.

- Difference Principle: Social and economic inequalities should be arranged to benefit the least advantaged members of society and provide fair equality of opportunity.

Libertarianism

Libertarianism emphasizes individual freedom and minimal state intervention. In terms of distributive justice, libertarians argue for the protection of property rights and voluntary exchanges. Key points include:

- Self-Ownership: Individuals have the right to control their own bodies and labor.

- Free Market: Resources should be distributed through free market mechanisms, with minimal state interference.

Psychological Foundations of Distributive Justice

Social Comparison

Social comparison theory suggests that individuals assess their well-being and fairness of distribution by comparing themselves to others. Key aspects include:

- Relative Deprivation: Feelings of injustice and dissatisfaction arise when individuals perceive that they have less than others, even if their absolute resources are adequate.

- Social Norms: Norms and cultural expectations influence perceptions of what constitutes a fair distribution.

Equity Theory

Equity theory posits that individuals seek a balance between their inputs (effort, skill, etc.) and outputs (rewards, recognition, etc.). Key components include:

- Input-Output Balance: People feel satisfied and perceive justice when their inputs are fairly rewarded.

- Restoring Equity: Individuals may take actions to restore perceived equity, such as reducing effort or demanding higher rewards if they feel under-compensated.

Procedural Justice

Procedural justice focuses on the fairness of the processes used to determine the distribution of resources. Key elements include:

- Fair Procedures: Ensuring that the processes for making distribution decisions are transparent, consistent, and unbiased.

- Voice and Participation: Allowing individuals to have a say in the decision-making process enhances their perceptions of fairness and acceptance of outcomes.

Implications for Social Equity

Addressing Inequality

Distributive justice plays a critical role in addressing social inequalities. By ensuring fair allocation of resources and opportunities, societies can:

- Reduce Poverty: Equitable distribution helps to alleviate poverty and ensure that everyone has access to basic necessities.

- Promote Social Mobility: Providing equal opportunities enables individuals from disadvantaged backgrounds to improve their socio-economic status.

- Enhance Social Cohesion: Fair distribution fosters a sense of community and trust, reducing social tensions and conflicts.

Policy and Practice

Governments and organizations can implement policies and practices to promote distributive justice, such as:

- Progressive Taxation: Implementing tax systems where higher earners contribute a larger share to fund public services and welfare programs.

- Social Safety Nets: Providing social safety nets, such as unemployment benefits, healthcare, and education, to ensure that basic needs are met for all.

- Affirmative Action: Implementing affirmative action policies to address historical and systemic inequalities and promote equal opportunities.

Criticisms and Challenges

Balancing Competing Principles

One of the main challenges in distributive justice is balancing competing principles, such as equality, merit, and need. This complexity can lead to:

- Policy Trade-offs: Policymakers must navigate trade-offs between different principles, such as maximizing overall welfare versus ensuring strict equality.

- Implementation Challenges: Practical implementation of distributive justice principles can be challenging due to economic, political, and social constraints.

Perceptions of Fairness

Perceptions of what constitutes a fair distribution can vary widely among individuals and cultures, leading to disagreements and conflicts. Addressing these perceptions requires:

- Cultural Sensitivity: Recognizing and respecting cultural differences in values and norms regarding distribution.

- Inclusive Dialogue: Facilitating inclusive dialogue to understand diverse perspectives and build consensus on fair distribution practices.

Distributive justice is a fundamental aspect of a just and equitable society, focusing on the fair allocation of resources and opportunities. By exploring various principles and theories, such as utilitarianism, egalitarianism, Rawls' theory of justice, and libertarianism, we gain a deeper understanding of the complexities and challenges involved in achieving distributive justice. The psychological foundations, including social comparison, equity theory, and procedural justice, provide insights into how individuals perceive and respond to distribution practices. Promoting distributive justice requires addressing inequalities, implementing fair policies, and navigating the challenges of balancing competing principles and diverse perceptions. As we continue to explore the psychological foundations of restorative justice in this book, the insights gained from understanding distributive justice will inform our broader discussion on creating a more just and compassionate society.

Restorative Justice: Repairing Harm and Restoring Relationships

Restorative justice represents a paradigm shift in how societies address crime and conflict. Unlike retributive justice, which focuses on punishment, restorative justice emphasizes repairing the harm caused by wrongdoing and restoring relationships among all parties involved—victims, offenders, and the community. This chapter explores the core principles, processes, and benefits of restorative justice, highlighting its transformative potential and practical applications.

Core Principles of Restorative Justice

Repairing Harm

The primary goal of restorative justice is to repair the harm caused by criminal behavior. This involves addressing the needs of victims, encouraging offenders to take responsibility, and engaging the community in the healing process.

- Victim-Centered Approach: Restorative justice prioritizes the needs and experiences of victims, providing them with a platform to express their feelings, ask questions, and receive reparation.

- Offender Accountability: Offenders are encouraged to understand the impact of their actions and actively participate in making amends.

- Community Involvement: The community plays a crucial role in supporting both victims and offenders, fostering a collective sense of responsibility for repairing harm.

Restoring Relationships

Restorative justice seeks to mend the broken relationships caused by crime. This process involves fostering empathy, understanding, and mutual respect among all parties.

- Dialogue and Communication: Facilitated dialogues allow victims and offenders to communicate directly, share their experiences, and work towards a shared understanding of the harm caused.

- Mutual Respect: All participants are treated with respect and dignity, ensuring that their voices are heard and valued.

- Reintegration: Efforts are made to reintegrate offenders into the community, helping them to build positive relationships and avoid reoffending.

Restorative Justice Processes

Victim-Offender Mediation

Process:

- Facilitated Meetings: A trained mediator facilitates meetings between the victim and the offender, providing a safe and structured environment for dialogue.

- Expression and Acknowledgment: Victims express their feelings and the impact of the crime, while offenders acknowledge their actions and take responsibility.

- Agreement and Reparation: Both parties work together to develop a mutually agreed-upon plan for reparation, which may include apologies, restitution, or community service.

Benefits:

- Empowerment and Healing: Victims feel heard and validated, which promotes emotional healing and closure.

- Accountability and Growth: Offenders gain insight into the consequences of their actions and are encouraged to make positive changes.

Family Group Conferencing

Process:

- Involving Families: Family group conferencing brings together the victim, the offender, their families, and other supporters in a structured meeting.

- Collaborative Planning: Participants collaboratively develop a plan to address the harm caused and support the offender's reintegration.

- Supportive Environment: The involvement of family members creates a supportive environment that enhances the effectiveness of the process.

Benefits:

- Comprehensive Support: Families provide emotional and practical support to both victims and offenders, facilitating holistic healing.

- Strengthening Bonds: The process strengthens family and community bonds, promoting collective responsibility and resilience.

Restorative Circles

Process:

- Circle Format: Participants sit in a circle and use a talking piece to ensure respectful and egalitarian dialogue.

- Inclusive Participation: Restorative circles involve a broader group of community members, fostering inclusive participation and shared decision-making.

- Collective Healing: The process focuses on collective healing, with all participants contributing to the resolution of the conflict and the development of reparation plans.

Benefits:

- Community Engagement: Restorative circles engage the community in addressing harm and supporting both victims and offenders.

- Empathy and Understanding: The inclusive nature of circles fosters empathy and understanding among participants, promoting social cohesion.

Benefits of Restorative Justice

For Victims

1. Emotional Healing:

- Voice and Validation: Victims have the opportunity to share their stories and feelings, receiving validation and support from the community and the offender.

- Sense of Closure: Direct communication with the offender can provide a sense of closure and peace, helping victims to move forward.

2. Empowerment:

- Active Participation: Victims actively participate in the justice process, influencing the outcomes and ensuring their needs are addressed.

- Restoration of Control: The process helps victims regain a sense of control over their lives, countering the powerlessness often felt after a crime.

For Offenders

1. Accountability and Growth:

- Understanding Impact: Offenders gain a deeper understanding of the impact of their actions, fostering genuine remorse and accountability.

- Personal Development: The process encourages offenders to take responsibility and make amends, promoting personal growth and positive behavioral change.

2. Reintegration and Support:

- Community Reintegration: Restorative justice supports the reintegration of offenders into the community, helping them build positive relationships and avoid reoffending.

- Support Systems: Offenders receive support from family, community members, and restorative justice practitioners, aiding their rehabilitation and reintegration.

For the Community

1. Strengthened Bonds:

- Collective Responsibility: Restorative justice fosters a sense of collective responsibility, with the community playing an active role in addressing harm and supporting both victims and offenders.

- Enhanced Cohesion: The process strengthens social bonds and promotes community cohesion, creating a more resilient and supportive community.

2. Preventing Future Harm:

- Addressing Root Causes: Restorative justice addresses the underlying causes of crime and conflict, promoting long-term solutions and preventing future harm.

- Building Trust: The process builds trust between community members and the justice system, enhancing social stability and safety.

Case Studies

Case Study 1: School-Based Restorative Justice

Background:

- A high school implemented restorative justice practices to address bullying and conflicts among students.

Implementation:

- The school used restorative circles to facilitate dialogues between affected students, involving teachers and parents as needed.

- Students participated in developing reparation plans, which included apologies, community service, and peer mentoring.

Outcomes:

- Bullying incidents decreased significantly, and students reported feeling safer and more supported.

- Relationships between students improved, fostering a positive and inclusive school climate.

Case Study 2: Community Restorative Justice Program

Background:

- A community-based restorative justice program was established to address low-level offenses and conflicts in a mid-sized city.

Implementation:

- The program used victim-offender mediation and family group conferencing to resolve conflicts and develop reparation plans.

- Community members were actively involved in supporting both victims and offenders, providing mentorship and resources.

Outcomes:

- Recidivism rates among participants dropped significantly, and community members reported increased trust in the justice system.

- The program enhanced community cohesion and resilience, with participants expressing greater empathy and understanding.

Challenges and Considerations

Emotional and Psychological Support

- Victim Support: Ensuring that victims receive adequate emotional and psychological support throughout the process is crucial for their healing and well-being.

- Offender Support: Providing support to offenders to help them manage feelings of shame, guilt, and fear is essential for their rehabilitation and reintegration.

Power Imbalances

- Addressing Imbalances: Facilitators must be skilled in recognizing and addressing power imbalances to ensure that all participants have an equal voice and that the process is fair and respectful.

- Inclusive Practices: Developing inclusive practices that empower marginalized or less assertive participants is vital for the success of restorative justice.

Cultural Sensitivity

- Cultural Competence: Facilitators and practitioners must be culturally competent, understanding and respecting the cultural backgrounds and norms of participants.

- Adaptation: Restorative justice practices should be adapted to fit the cultural context of the community, ensuring relevance and effectiveness.

Restorative justice offers a powerful alternative to traditional retributive justice systems, focusing on repairing harm and restoring relationships. By prioritizing the needs of victims, encouraging offender accountability, and involving the community, restorative justice promotes healing, empathy, and social cohesion. Understanding the core principles, processes, and benefits of restorative justice is essential for its successful implementation and widespread adoption. As we continue to explore restorative justice in this book, the insights gained from this chapter will provide a solid foundation for understanding its transformative potential and practical applications.

Cognitive Dissonance Theory: Understanding How Offenders Reconcile Their Actions with Their Self-Image

Introduction

Cognitive dissonance theory, a cornerstone of social psychology, provides valuable insights into the psychological processes that underpin restorative justice. Developed by Leon Festinger in the 1950s, cognitive dissonance theory explores the discomfort individuals experience when they hold conflicting beliefs or when their actions contradict their self-image. This chapter delves into the principles of cognitive dissonance theory, its relevance to restorative justice, and how it can be leveraged to facilitate offender rehabilitation and reconciliation.

Principles of Cognitive Dissonance Theory

Cognitive Dissonance

Cognitive dissonance occurs when an individual experiences psychological discomfort due to holding two or more conflicting cognitions. These cognitions can be beliefs, attitudes, or behaviors. Key aspects include:

- Inconsistency: The core of cognitive dissonance is the inconsistency between an individual's beliefs and actions or between different beliefs.

- Discomfort: This inconsistency leads to psychological discomfort, motivating the individual to reduce the dissonance and achieve cognitive harmony.

Dissonance Reduction

Individuals are motivated to reduce cognitive dissonance through various strategies, including:

- Changing Beliefs: Altering existing beliefs to align with actions or new information.

- Changing Actions: Modifying behaviors to be consistent with beliefs and values.

- Adding Cognitions: Introducing new cognitions that justify or rationalize the conflicting beliefs or behaviors.

- Trivializing: Downplaying the importance of the conflicting cognitions to reduce their impact.

Cognitive Dissonance in the Context of Offending

Offender Self-Image

Offenders often face significant cognitive dissonance due to the conflict between their self-image and their criminal actions. This dissonance can manifest in several ways:

- Moral Self-Concept: Most individuals view themselves as moral and decent. Committing a crime conflicts with this self-concept, creating cognitive dissonance.

- Rationalization: Offenders may rationalize their actions to reduce dissonance, convincing themselves that their behavior was justified or unavoidable.

Dissonance Reduction Strategies Among Offenders

Offenders employ various strategies to reduce the dissonance between their self-image and their actions:

- Denial: Denying responsibility for the crime or minimizing its impact.

- Justification: Justifying the crime by blaming external circumstances or the victim.

- Attitude Change: Altering their attitudes towards the crime, viewing it as less severe or wrong.

Relevance of Cognitive Dissonance Theory to Restorative Justice

Facilitating Offender Accountability

Restorative justice leverages cognitive dissonance to encourage offenders to confront and reconcile their actions with their self-image:

- Acknowledging Harm: By participating in restorative justice processes, offenders are encouraged to acknowledge the harm they have caused, increasing cognitive dissonance and prompting self-reflection.

- Responsibility and Remorse: Confronting the victim and understanding the impact of their actions can lead offenders to accept responsibility and feel genuine remorse, essential steps for dissonance reduction.

Promoting Behavior Change

Cognitive dissonance can be a powerful motivator for behavior change. Restorative justice processes create conditions that enhance this motivation:

- Consistency with Self-Image: Offenders are motivated to align their actions with their self-image as moral individuals, leading to positive behavioral changes.

- Commitment to Reparation: Developing reparation plans that include actions consistent with positive self-concepts, such as making amends and community service, helps offenders reduce dissonance through constructive behavior.

Applying Cognitive Dissonance Theory in Restorative Justice Practices

Victim-Offender Mediation

Process:

- Facilitated Dialogue: Mediators facilitate a dialogue between the victim and the offender, allowing the offender to hear firsthand the impact of their actions.

- Acknowledge Harm: Offenders are encouraged to acknowledge the harm they have caused, increasing cognitive dissonance and prompting self-reflection.

- Commitment to Change: Offenders make commitments to change their behavior and make amends, aligning their actions with their self-image as moral individuals.

Benefits:

- Empathy Development: Understanding the victim's perspective fosters empathy and reduces dissonance.

- Behavioral Alignment: Offenders' commitments to positive actions help align their behavior with their self-image, promoting long-term change.

Family Group Conferencing

Process:

- Inclusive Meetings: Family group conferencing involves the offender, the victim, their families, and other supporters in a structured meeting.

- Shared Responsibility: Participants collaboratively develop a plan to address the harm caused and support the offender's reintegration.

- Supportive Environment: The involvement of family and community members creates a supportive environment for dissonance reduction and behavior change.

Benefits:

- Holistic Support: Family and community support enhances the offender's commitment to positive change.

- Collective Accountability: The process fosters a sense of collective responsibility and accountability, reinforcing the offender's motivation to reduce dissonance through constructive behavior.

Case Studies

Case Study 1: Youth Offender Program

Background:

- A restorative justice program for youth offenders was implemented in a mid-sized city to address juvenile delinquency.

Implementation:

- The program used victim-offender mediation to facilitate dialogues between offenders and their victims.

- Offenders participated in developing reparation plans that included apologies, restitution, and community service.

Outcomes:

- Offenders reported increased empathy and understanding of the impact of their actions.

- Recidivism rates among participants dropped significantly, and offenders demonstrated positive behavioral changes.

Analysis:

- The program effectively leveraged cognitive dissonance to promote offender accountability and behavior change.

- The supportive environment and structured reparation plans helped offenders align their actions with their self-image, reducing dissonance.

Case Study 2: Domestic Violence Restorative Program

Background:

- A restorative justice program was introduced to address domestic violence cases in a suburban community.

Implementation:

- The program included family group conferencing to involve victims, offenders, their families, and community members in the healing process.

- Offenders participated in therapy sessions and developed reparation plans to make amends and change their behavior.

Outcomes:

- Victims reported a sense of empowerment and emotional healing, while offenders showed increased accountability and reduced reoffending rates.

- The program enhanced community cohesion and resilience, with participants expressing greater empathy and understanding.

Analysis:

- The program successfully used cognitive dissonance to encourage offenders to confront the impact of their actions and commit to positive change.

- The involvement of family and community members provided a supportive environment for dissonance reduction and behavioral alignment.

Challenges and Considerations

Emotional and Psychological Support

- Offender Support: Providing emotional and psychological support to offenders is crucial for helping them manage the discomfort of cognitive dissonance and make positive changes.

- Victim Support: Ensuring that victims receive adequate support throughout the restorative justice process is essential for their healing and well-being.

Facilitator Training

- Cognitive Dissonance Awareness: Training facilitators to understand cognitive dissonance and its role in restorative justice can enhance their effectiveness in guiding the process.

- Empathy and Communication Skills: Facilitators should be skilled in fostering empathy and facilitating open, respectful communication between participants.

Cognitive dissonance theory offers valuable insights into the psychological processes that underpin restorative justice. By leveraging cognitive dissonance, restorative justice encourages offenders to confront the impact of their actions, reconcile their behavior with their self-image, and commit to positive change. Understanding the principles and applications of cognitive dissonance theory is essential for practitioners to design effective restorative justice processes that promote healing, accountability, and long-term behavioral change. As we continue to explore the psychological foundations of restorative justice in this book, the insights gained from cognitive dissonance theory will inform our broader discussion on creating a more just and compassionate society.

Empathy and Altruism: The Role of Empathy in Fostering Understanding and Reconciliation

Empathy and altruism are crucial psychological concepts that underpin restorative justice. Empathy, the ability to understand and share the feelings of another, plays a vital role in fostering understanding and reconciliation between victims and offenders. Altruism, the selfless concern for the well-being of others, further enhances the restorative process by promoting actions that benefit others without expecting anything in return. This chapter delves into the principles of empathy and altruism, their significance in restorative justice, and practical applications to enhance the effectiveness of restorative practices.

Understanding Empathy

Definition and Types of Empathy

Empathy involves recognizing, understanding, and sharing the emotions of others. It is a multifaceted construct comprising different types:

- Cognitive Empathy: The ability to understand another person's perspective or mental state. It involves recognizing and comprehending the emotions of others.

- Emotional Empathy: The ability to share the feelings of another person, often leading to emotional resonance and affective responses.

- Compassionate Empathy: The ability to understand and share the feelings of others, coupled with a desire to help alleviate their suffering.

The Neuroscience of Empathy

Recent advancements in neuroscience have provided insights into the brain mechanisms underlying empathy:

- Mirror Neurons: Mirror neurons are specialized cells in the brain that fire both when an individual performs an action and when they observe someone else performing the same action. These neurons play a crucial role in empathy by enabling individuals to simulate and understand the emotions and actions of others.

- Empathy Circuits: The brain's empathy circuits involve regions such as the anterior insula, anterior cingulate cortex, and prefrontal cortex, which are activated when individuals experience or observe emotions.

The Role of Empathy in Restorative Justice

Fostering Understanding and Connection

Empathy is fundamental to the restorative justice process, as it facilitates understanding and connection between victims, offenders, and the community:

- Victim-Offender Dialogue: Empathy allows offenders to understand the impact of their actions on victims, fostering genuine remorse and accountability. For victims, empathy enables them to see the offender's perspective and recognize the circumstances that may have contributed to the crime.

- Building Bridges: Empathy helps bridge the gap between victims and offenders, creating a foundation for open communication, mutual understanding, and reconciliation.

Promoting Emotional Healing

Empathy plays a crucial role in promoting emotional healing for both victims and offenders:

- Victims: When victims feel that their emotions are understood and validated by the offender and the community, it can lead to emotional release and healing. Empathy helps victims regain a sense of dignity and control over their lives.

- Offenders: Empathy encourages offenders to confront the emotional consequences of their actions, fostering self-awareness and personal growth. This process is essential for genuine remorse and long-term rehabilitation.

Understanding Altruism

Definition and Types of Altruism

Altruism involves selfless concern for the well-being of others, often leading to actions that benefit others without expecting anything in return. Key types include:

- Reciprocal Altruism: Actions taken with the expectation that the favor will be returned in the future.

- Pure Altruism: Selfless actions performed solely for the benefit of others, without any expectation of personal gain.

- Kin Altruism: Altruistic behaviors directed towards close relatives, ensuring the survival and success of shared genes.

The Psychology of Altruism

The psychological basis of altruism involves several factors:

- Innate Tendencies: Humans have evolved innate tendencies towards altruistic behavior, which enhances social cohesion and mutual support within communities.

- Moral Development: Altruistic behavior is influenced by moral development, with individuals who have a strong sense of moral values and empathy more likely to engage in selfless acts.

- Social and Cultural Influences: Social and cultural norms, values, and practices shape altruistic behavior, promoting actions that benefit others and contribute to the common good.

The Role of Altruism in Restorative Justice

Encouraging Positive Actions

Altruism enhances the restorative justice process by encouraging positive actions that benefit victims, offenders, and the community:

- Offender Reparation: Altruistic actions by offenders, such as making amends, performing community service, or providing restitution, demonstrate genuine remorse and a commitment to repair the harm caused.

- Community Support: Community members who engage in altruistic behavior, such as volunteering in restorative justice programs or supporting victims and offenders, contribute to the overall success and sustainability of the process.

Strengthening Community Bonds

Altruism strengthens community bonds by fostering a sense of mutual support and collective responsibility:

- Collective Healing: Altruistic actions promote collective healing by addressing the needs of victims, supporting offender rehabilitation, and enhancing community cohesion.

- Building Trust: Altruism helps build trust within the community, as individuals see others acting selflessly for the common good. This trust is essential for maintaining social harmony and preventing future conflicts.

Practical Applications in Restorative Justice

Facilitating Empathy Development

Restorative justice practices can be designed to facilitate empathy development among participants:

- Victim Impact Statements: Allowing victims to share their experiences and the impact of the crime can evoke empathy in offenders, helping them understand the emotional and psychological consequences of their actions.

- Role-Playing Exercises: Facilitators can use role-playing exercises to help offenders and community members step into the shoes of victims, fostering empathy and understanding.

Encouraging Altruistic Behavior

Restorative justice programs can encourage altruistic behavior through various strategies:

- Community Service Projects: Involving offenders in community service projects allows them to give back to the community and demonstrate their commitment to positive change.

- Restitution Plans: Developing restitution plans that include altruistic actions, such as helping victims or contributing to community initiatives, promotes a sense of responsibility and collective well-being.

Case Studies

Case Study 1: Empathy Development in Youth Offenders

Background:

- A restorative justice program for youth offenders was implemented to address bullying and conflicts in a high school.

Implementation:

- The program included victim-offender dialogues and empathy-building exercises, such as role-playing and group discussions.

- Offenders participated in community service projects as part of their reparation plans.

Outcomes:

- Offenders reported increased empathy and understanding of the impact of their actions on victims.

- The program led to reduced bullying incidents and improved relationships among students.

Analysis:

- The program effectively leveraged empathy and altruism to promote positive behavior change and strengthen community bonds.

- Empathy-building exercises and community service projects enhanced the offenders' sense of responsibility and commitment to making amends.

Case Study 2: Altruism in Community Restorative Justice

Background:

- A community-based restorative justice program was established to address low-level offenses and conflicts in a mid-sized city.

Implementation:

- The program involved victim-offender mediation, family group conferencing, and community restorative circles.

- Community members volunteered in the program, providing support to victims and offenders and participating in collective reparation efforts.

Outcomes:

- The program enhanced community cohesion and trust, with participants expressing greater empathy and understanding.

- Recidivism rates among offenders dropped significantly, and victims reported a sense of empowerment and healing.

Analysis:

- The program successfully harnessed altruism to support the restorative justice process, fostering a culture of mutual support and collective responsibility.

- The involvement of community volunteers and the emphasis on altruistic actions contributed to the program's overall effectiveness and sustainability.

Challenges and Considerations

Overcoming Resistance

- Emotional Resistance: Some participants, particularly offenders, may initially resist empathizing with victims or engaging in altruistic actions. Facilitators must be skilled in creating a safe and supportive environment that encourages openness and emotional vulnerability.

- Cultural Differences: Cultural differences can influence the expression and reception of empathy and altruism. Practitioners must be culturally competent and adaptable to ensure that restorative practices are inclusive and respectful of diverse backgrounds.

Sustaining Altruism

- Motivation: Sustaining altruistic behavior over time requires ongoing motivation and support. Restorative justice programs should include mechanisms for recognizing and rewarding positive actions, such as public acknowledgment or certificates of appreciation.

- Community Engagement: Continuous community engagement is essential for maintaining a culture of altruism and mutual support. Regular community events, workshops, and training sessions can help reinforce the values of empathy and altruism.

Empathy and altruism are fundamental to the success of restorative justice, fostering understanding, reconciliation, and positive behavior change. By leveraging empathy, restorative justice encourages offenders to confront the impact of their actions and develop genuine remorse. Altruism enhances the process by promoting selfless actions that benefit victims, offenders, and the community, strengthening social bonds and collective well-being. Understanding the principles and applications of empathy and altruism is crucial for designing effective restorative justice programs that promote healing, accountability, and long-term social harmony. As we continue to explore the psychological foundations of restorative justice in this book, the insights gained from empathy and altruism will inform our broader discussion on creating a more just and compassionate society.

Social Learning Theory: How Behaviors Are Influenced by Observing and Interacting with Others

Introduction

Social Learning Theory (SLT), developed by Albert Bandura, provides a comprehensive framework for understanding how behaviors are learned and modified through observing and interacting with others. This theory has significant implications for restorative justice, as it highlights the importance of social environments and interactions in shaping behavior. This chapter explores the principles of Social Learning Theory, its relevance to restorative justice, and practical applications to enhance the effectiveness of restorative practices.

Principles of Social Learning Theory

Observational Learning

Observational learning, or modeling, is a core component of Social Learning Theory. It posits that individuals can learn new behaviors by watching others, rather than through direct experience alone.

- Attention: For observational learning to occur, individuals must pay attention to the behavior being modeled. Factors such as the model's attractiveness, competence, and status can influence attention.

- Retention: Individuals must remember the observed behavior to replicate it later. This involves encoding the behavior into memory.

- Reproduction: The ability to reproduce the observed behavior depends on physical and cognitive capabilities.

- Motivation: Motivation to imitate the behavior is influenced by anticipated rewards or punishments, which can be direct or vicarious.

Vicarious Reinforcement and Punishment

Vicarious reinforcement and punishment refer to learning that occurs by observing the consequences of others' actions. Individuals are more likely to imitate behaviors that are rewarded and avoid behaviors that are punished.

- Vicarious Reinforcement: Observing a model receive rewards for a behavior increases the likelihood that the observer will imitate the behavior.

- Vicarious Punishment: Observing a model receive punishment for a behavior decreases the likelihood that the observer will imitate the behavior.

Self-Efficacy

Self-efficacy, or the belief in one's ability to succeed in specific situations, is another crucial aspect of Social Learning Theory. Higher self-efficacy can enhance motivation and the likelihood of adopting new behaviors.

- Sources of Self-Efficacy: Self-efficacy is influenced by personal experiences, vicarious experiences (observing others), verbal persuasion (encouragement from others), and physiological states (emotional arousal).

Relevance of Social Learning Theory to Restorative Justice

Modeling Positive Behaviors

Restorative justice processes can utilize modeling to encourage positive behaviors among participants:

- Role Models: Facilitators, community leaders, and peers can serve as positive role models, demonstrating behaviors such as empathy, accountability, and constructive conflict resolution.

- Restorative Practices: Engaging in restorative practices themselves, such as dialogue and mediation, can serve as a model for effective communication and problem-solving.

Vicarious Learning

Vicarious learning can play a significant role in restorative justice by influencing participants' behaviors through observed consequences:

- Positive Reinforcement: Observing positive outcomes, such as reconciliation and community support, can reinforce constructive behaviors among offenders and community members.

- Negative Consequences: Observing the negative consequences of harmful behaviors, such as social disapproval or loss of trust, can deter individuals from engaging in similar actions.

Enhancing Self-Efficacy

Restorative justice can enhance participants' self-efficacy, increasing their confidence in their ability to change and make amends:

- Supportive Environment: Creating a supportive environment where participants feel encouraged and capable of change can boost self-efficacy.

- Skill-Building Activities: Providing opportunities for skill-building, such as communication and problem-solving workshops, can enhance participants' confidence and competence.

Practical Applications in Restorative Justice

Victim-Offender Mediation

Process:

- Facilitated Dialogue: Mediators facilitate a dialogue between the victim and the offender, modeling effective communication and empathy.

- Behavioral Modeling: Offenders observe the mediators and victims demonstrating positive behaviors such as active listening, expressing feelings constructively, and seeking resolution.

Benefits:

- Learning through Observation: Offenders learn through observation, understanding the impact of their actions and the importance of making amends.

- Motivation to Change: Observing positive outcomes from the mediation process can motivate offenders to adopt constructive behaviors.

Community Restorative Circles

Process:

- Inclusive Participation: Restorative circles involve victims, offenders, and community members in a structured dialogue, promoting mutual understanding and collective problem-solving.

- Role Modeling: Community members and facilitators model behaviors such as respect, empathy, and accountability during the circle process.

Benefits:

- Social Learning: Participants learn from observing others' positive behaviors, reinforcing the adoption of similar behaviors.

- Community Support: The collective nature of restorative circles provides a support system, enhancing participants' self-efficacy and commitment to positive change.

Case Studies

Case Study 1: School-Based Restorative Justice Program

Background:

- A high school implemented a restorative justice program to address conflicts and bullying among students.

Implementation:

- The program included restorative circles and peer mediation, with trained facilitators and student leaders modeling positive behaviors.

- Students participated in skill-building workshops to enhance their communication and conflict resolution abilities.

Outcomes:

- Incidents of bullying and conflicts decreased significantly, and students reported improved relationships and a more positive school climate.

- Students demonstrated increased empathy, accountability, and self-efficacy, attributing these changes to the observed behaviors and supportive environment.

Analysis:

- The program effectively utilized Social Learning Theory principles, with role modeling and vicarious learning playing key roles in behavior change.

- Enhancing self-efficacy through skill-building and supportive interactions contributed to the program's success.

Case Study 2: Community-Based Restorative Justice Program

Background:

- A community-based restorative justice program was established to address low-level offenses and conflicts in a diverse urban neighborhood.

Implementation:

- The program involved community restorative circles, victim-offender mediation, and community service projects, with facilitators and community leaders modeling positive behaviors.

- Offenders and community members participated in workshops and training sessions to build skills and confidence.

Outcomes:

- The program led to reduced recidivism rates among offenders, improved community relationships, and increased trust in the justice system.

- Participants reported greater empathy, accountability, and self-efficacy, influenced by observed behaviors and positive reinforcement.

Analysis:

- The program successfully applied Social Learning Theory, with observational learning and vicarious reinforcement driving behavior change.

- Enhancing self-efficacy through supportive interactions and skill-building activities played a crucial role in the program's effectiveness.

Challenges and Considerations

Ensuring Effective Modeling

- Consistency: Role models must consistently demonstrate positive behaviors to effectively influence participants.

- Credibility: Role models should be credible and respected by participants to maximize their impact.

Addressing Resistance to Change

- Overcoming Skepticism: Some participants may be skeptical or resistant to adopting new behaviors. Facilitators must create a safe and supportive environment that encourages openness and willingness to change.

- Tailoring Interventions: Interventions should be tailored to the specific needs and contexts of participants, recognizing that individual differences can influence learning and behavior change.

Sustaining Behavior Change

- Ongoing Support: Sustaining behavior change requires ongoing support and reinforcement. Restorative justice programs should include mechanisms for continuous engagement and encouragement.

- Community Involvement: Engaging the broader community in restorative justice efforts helps sustain positive behaviors and fosters a culture of mutual support and accountability.

Social Learning Theory offers valuable insights into how behaviors are influenced by observing and interacting with others, making it highly relevant to restorative justice. By leveraging principles such as observational learning, vicarious reinforcement, and self-efficacy, restorative justice programs can effectively promote positive behavior change and foster understanding and reconciliation. Understanding and applying these principles is crucial for designing restorative justice processes that maximize their impact and contribute to a more just and compassionate society. As we continue to explore the psychological foundations of restorative justice in this book, the insights gained from Social Learning Theory will inform our broader discussion on creating effective and transformative restorative practices.

CHAPTER 04

EMOTIONAL EFEEECTS OF PARTICIPANTS

Emotional Healing for Victims

Restorative justice offers victims of crime a unique opportunity for emotional healing, which is often absent in traditional justice systems. By providing a platform for victims to express their feelings and receive apologies from offenders, restorative justice addresses the emotional and psychological needs of victims, fostering a sense of closure, empowerment, and validation. This chapter explores the various dimensions of emotional healing for victims within the restorative justice framework, highlighting the processes and benefits that contribute to their recovery.

The Need for Emotional Healing

Impact of Crime on Victims

Crime can have profound and lasting emotional and psychological impacts on victims. These impacts include:

- Trauma and Anxiety: Victims often experience trauma, anxiety, and fear following a crime, which can disrupt their daily lives and mental health.

- Loss of Control: Crime can leave victims feeling powerless and vulnerable, with a diminished sense of control over their lives.

- Anger and Resentment: Victims may harbor feelings of anger and resentment towards the offender, which can hinder their ability to move forward.

Limitations of Traditional Justice Systems

Traditional justice systems often focus on punishing the offender rather than addressing the needs of the victim. This approach can leave victims feeling neglected and dissatisfied:

- Lack of Voice: Victims may feel that their voices are not heard in the judicial process, as they have limited opportunities to express their feelings or influence the outcome.

- Inadequate Closure: The emphasis on punishment over reparation can fail to provide victims with a sense of closure and healing.

Restorative Justice and Emotional Healing

Opportunities for Expression

Restorative justice prioritizes the emotional and psychological well-being of victims by providing them with opportunities to express their feelings and experiences:

- Victim Impact Statements: Victims are encouraged to share their stories and describe the impact of the crime on their lives. This process allows victims to articulate their emotions and experiences in a supportive environment.

- Facilitated Dialogues: During restorative justice processes such as victim-offender mediation or restorative circles, victims have the opportunity to engage in direct dialogue with the offender, expressing their feelings and asking questions.

Receiving Apologies

Receiving a sincere apology from the offender can be a crucial component of emotional healing for victims:

- Acknowledgment of Harm: A sincere apology from the offender acknowledges the harm caused and validates the victim's experiences. This acknowledgment is essential for victims to feel heard and understood.

- Fostering Forgiveness: While forgiveness is not always the goal, receiving an apology can help some victims move towards forgiveness, releasing negative emotions and fostering emotional healing.

Processes Facilitating Emotional Healing

Victim-Offender Mediation

Process:

- Preparation: Before the mediation, facilitators work with both the victim and the offender to prepare them for the dialogue. This preparation includes discussing expectations, addressing concerns, and providing emotional support.

- Facilitated Dialogue: During the mediation, a trained facilitator guides the conversation, allowing the victim to express their feelings and the offender to respond. The dialogue focuses on understanding the impact of the crime and discussing ways to make amends.

Benefits:

- Emotional Release: Victims have the opportunity to express their emotions and experiences, leading to emotional release and relief.

- Validation: The acknowledgment of harm by the offender provides victims with validation and a sense of justice.

Restorative Circles

Process:

- Inclusive Participation: Restorative circles involve victims, offenders, and community members in a collective dialogue. Participants sit in a circle, using a talking piece to ensure respectful and egalitarian communication.

- Shared Stories: Victims share their stories and feelings, while other participants listen and respond with empathy and support.

Benefits:

- Community Support: The presence of supportive community members provides victims with a sense of solidarity and validation.

- Holistic Healing: The inclusive nature of restorative circles promotes holistic healing by addressing the emotional, psychological, and social dimensions of the victim's experience.

Family Group Conferencing

Process:

- Involving Families: Family group conferencing brings together the victim, the offender, their families, and other supporters in a structured meeting.

- Collaborative Dialogue: Participants engage in a collaborative dialogue to discuss the impact of the crime and develop a plan for reparation and support.

Benefits:

- Supportive Environment: The involvement of family members creates a supportive and empathetic environment for the victim.

- Empowerment: Victims are actively involved in the decision-making process, enhancing their sense of empowerment and control.

Benefits of Emotional Healing

Sense of Closure

Restorative justice processes provide victims with a sense of closure by addressing the emotional and psychological dimensions of their experience:

- Resolution: By engaging in dialogue and receiving an apology, victims can achieve a sense of resolution and peace.

- Moving Forward: The process helps victims move forward with their lives, reducing feelings of anger, resentment, and fear.

Empowerment

Restorative justice empowers victims by giving them a central role in the justice process:

- Voice and Influence: Victims have the opportunity to express their feelings and influence the outcome, restoring a sense of control and agency.

- Active Participation: Active participation in the process enhances victims' self-esteem and confidence, contributing to their overall well-being.

Validation of Experiences

Validation is a critical component of emotional healing for victims:

- Acknowledgment: The acknowledgment of harm by the offender and the community validates the victim's experiences and emotions.

- Support: The support and empathy of facilitators, community members, and family provide victims with a sense of validation and solidarity.

Case Studies

Case Study 1: Victim-Offender Mediation for Theft

Background:

- A restorative justice program was implemented to address theft cases in a suburban community.

Implementation:

- The program included victim-offender mediation sessions, where victims and offenders engaged in facilitated dialogues.

- Victims shared their stories and the impact of the theft on their lives, while offenders listened and responded with apologies and reparation plans.

Outcomes:

- Victims reported a sense of closure and emotional relief after expressing their feelings and receiving apologies from the offenders.

- Offenders demonstrated increased empathy and accountability, contributing to their rehabilitation.

Analysis:

- The program effectively facilitated emotional healing for victims by providing opportunities for expression and acknowledgment of harm.

- The supportive and empathetic environment of the mediation sessions enhanced the victims' sense of validation and empowerment.

Case Study 2: Restorative Circle for Assault

Background:

- A restorative justice program was introduced to address assault cases in a high school setting.

Implementation:

- The program involved restorative circles, where victims, offenders, and community members participated in a collective dialogue.

- Victims shared their experiences and feelings, while other participants listened and provided support.

Outcomes:

- Victims reported feeling heard and validated, with a sense of closure and reduced anxiety.

- The process fostered empathy and understanding among participants, promoting a positive and inclusive school climate.

Analysis:

- The restorative circles successfully facilitated emotional healing for victims by creating a supportive and inclusive environment.

- The presence of community members and peers provided additional validation and solidarity, enhancing the victims' sense of well-being.

Challenges and Considerations

Emotional Readiness

- Assessing Readiness: Ensuring that victims are emotionally ready to participate in restorative justice processes is crucial for their well-being. Facilitators must assess readiness and provide appropriate support.

- Voluntary Participation: Participation in restorative justice processes should be entirely voluntary, with victims free to withdraw at any time if they feel uncomfortable or distressed.

Cultural Sensitivity

- Cultural Competence: Facilitators must be culturally competent, understanding and respecting the cultural backgrounds and norms of participants.

- Adaptation: Restorative justice practices should be adapted to fit the cultural context of the community, ensuring relevance and effectiveness.

Ongoing Support

- Continuous Support: Providing ongoing emotional and psychological support to victims throughout and after the restorative justice process is essential for sustained healing.

- Access to Resources: Ensuring that victims have access to resources such as counseling, therapy, and support groups can enhance their recovery and well-being.

Emotional healing is a fundamental component of restorative justice, offering victims opportunities to express their feelings, receive apologies, and achieve a sense of closure and empowerment. By prioritizing the emotional and psychological needs of victims, restorative justice fosters validation and support, addressing the limitations of traditional justice systems. Understanding the processes and benefits of emotional healing is crucial for designing effective restorative justice programs that promote holistic recovery and well-being. As we continue to explore the emotional effects of restorative justice on participants in this book, the insights gained from emotional healing will inform our broader discussion on creating a more just and compassionate society.

Empowerment: How Participation in the Process Can Restore a Sense of Control

Introduction

Empowerment is a key emotional benefit of restorative justice for victims. The traditional justice system often leaves victims feeling powerless and voiceless, but restorative justice provides a platform for active participation, allowing victims to regain a sense of control over their lives. This chapter explores the concept of empowerment in the context of restorative justice, examining how participation in the process restores control and enhances the emotional and psychological well-being of victims.

Understanding Empowerment

Definition and Dimensions of Empowerment

Empowerment is the process of gaining control, authority, and influence over one's life and the decisions that affect it. It involves several dimensions:

- Psychological Empowerment: Enhancing self-esteem, confidence, and a sense of personal efficacy.

- Social Empowerment: Improving social connections, support networks, and the ability to influence social outcomes.

- Political Empowerment: Gaining influence over political processes and decisions that affect one's life and community.

Importance of Empowerment for Victims

Empowerment is crucial for victims of crime as it helps counteract the feelings of helplessness, vulnerability, and powerlessness that often accompany victimization:

- Restoring Agency: Empowerment restores victims' sense of agency and control over their lives, helping them to actively participate in their recovery.

- Enhancing Resilience: Empowered victims are better equipped to cope with the emotional and psychological aftermath of crime, enhancing their resilience and overall well-being.

Mechanisms of Empowerment in Restorative Justice

Active Participation

Restorative justice processes involve active participation by victims, giving them a central role in the resolution of their cases:

- Voice and Expression: Victims have the opportunity to express their feelings, experiences, and needs directly, ensuring that their voices are heard and valued.

- Influence and Decision-Making: Victims actively participate in decision-making, influencing the outcomes of the restorative process, including reparation plans and agreements.

Validation and Support

Restorative justice provides validation and support to victims, reinforcing their sense of worth and importance:

- Acknowledgment of Harm: Offenders and the community acknowledge the harm caused to the victim, validating their experiences and emotions.

- Emotional Support: Facilitators, community members, and support networks provide emotional support, enhancing victims' sense of belonging and solidarity.

Processes Facilitating Empowerment

Victim-Offender Mediation

Process:

- Preparation: Facilitators prepare victims for the mediation process, discussing their expectations, concerns, and desired outcomes.

- Facilitated Dialogue: During mediation, victims engage in a structured dialogue with the offender, expressing their feelings and influencing the resolution process.

Benefits:

- Restored Control: Victims regain a sense of control over the justice process by actively participating and influencing the outcomes.

- Enhanced Confidence: The opportunity to express their feelings and receive acknowledgment boosts victims' confidence and self-esteem.

Restorative Circles

Process:

- Inclusive Participation: Restorative circles involve victims, offenders, and community members in a collective dialogue, ensuring that all voices are heard and respected.

- Shared Decision-Making: Participants collaboratively develop reparation plans and agreements, with victims playing a key role in shaping the outcomes.

Benefits:

- Collective Empowerment: The inclusive nature of restorative circles fosters a sense of collective empowerment, with victims feeling supported and validated by the community.

- Social Connections: Participation in restorative circles enhances victims' social connections and support networks, contributing to their overall empowerment.

Family Group Conferencing

Process:

- Involving Families: Family group conferencing involves victims, offenders, their families, and other supporters in a structured meeting to discuss the impact of the crime and develop a plan for reparation and support.

- Collaborative Dialogue: The process emphasizes collaborative dialogue and decision-making, with victims actively participating and influencing the outcomes.

Benefits:

- Supportive Environment: The involvement of family members creates a supportive and empathetic environment, enhancing victims' sense of empowerment.

- Enhanced Agency: Victims regain a sense of agency and control by participating in the decision-making process and influencing the outcomes.

Benefits of Empowerment

Psychological Benefits

Empowerment through restorative justice has significant psychological benefits for victims:

- Increased Self-Esteem: Active participation and validation boost victims' self-esteem and confidence.

- Reduced Anxiety: Regaining control over the justice process reduces feelings of anxiety and helplessness.

- Emotional Healing: Empowerment facilitates emotional healing by addressing the psychological and emotional needs of victims.

Social Benefits

Empowerment also has important social benefits for victims:

- Improved Social Connections: Participation in restorative justice enhances victims' social connections and support networks.

- Community Integration: Empowered victims are better integrated into their communities, fostering a sense of belonging and social cohesion.

- Collective Resilience: Empowerment contributes to collective resilience, with communities working together to support victims and address the harm caused by crime.

Case Studies

Case Study 1: Victim-Offender Mediation for Burglary

Background:

- A restorative justice program was implemented to address burglary cases in an urban community.

Implementation:

- The program included victim-offender mediation sessions, where victims and offenders engaged in facilitated dialogues.

- Victims expressed their feelings and needs, while offenders acknowledged the harm caused and developed reparation plans.

Outcomes:

- Victims reported increased self-esteem and a sense of control over the justice process.

- The acknowledgment of harm and the development of reparation plans contributed to victims' emotional healing and empowerment.

Analysis:

- The program effectively facilitated empowerment by providing opportunities for active participation and validation.

- The supportive environment of the mediation sessions enhanced victims' sense of control and confidence.

Case Study 2: Restorative Circle for Assault

Background:

- A restorative justice program was introduced to address assault cases in a high school setting.

Implementation:

- The program involved restorative circles, where victims, offenders, and community members participated in a collective dialogue.

- Victims shared their experiences and feelings, while other participants listened and provided support.

Outcomes:

- Victims reported feeling heard and empowered, with a sense of control over the justice process.

- The process fostered empathy and understanding among participants, promoting a positive and inclusive school climate.

Analysis:

- The restorative circles successfully facilitated empowerment by creating an inclusive and supportive environment.

- The active participation and social support provided by the community enhanced victims' sense of empowerment and well-being.

Challenges and Considerations

Ensuring Voluntary Participation

- Voluntary Nature: Participation in restorative justice processes should be entirely voluntary, with victims free to withdraw at any time if they feel uncomfortable or distressed.

- Informed Consent: Facilitators must ensure that victims fully understand the process and its potential benefits and challenges before agreeing to participate.

Addressing Power Imbalances

- Facilitator Training: Facilitators must be trained to recognize and address power imbalances, ensuring that all participants have an equal voice and that the process is fair and respectful.

- Empowering Marginalized Voices: Developing inclusive practices that empower marginalized or less assertive participants is vital for the success of restorative justice.

Providing Ongoing Support

- Continuous Support: Providing ongoing emotional and psychological support to victims throughout and after the restorative justice process is essential for sustained empowerment.

- Access to Resources: Ensuring that victims have access to resources such as counseling, therapy, and support groups can enhance their recovery and well-being.

Empowerment is a fundamental component of restorative justice, offering victims the opportunity to regain a sense of control and actively participate in the justice process. By providing platforms for expression, validation, and decision-making, restorative justice enhances victims' psychological and social well-being, addressing the limitations of traditional justice systems. Understanding the mechanisms and benefits of empowerment is crucial for designing effective restorative justice programs that promote holistic recovery and well-being. As we continue to explore the emotional effects of restorative justice on participants in this book, the insights gained from empowerment will inform our broader discussion on creating a more just and compassionate society.

Accountability: Understanding the Impact of Their Actions and Taking Responsibility

Introduction

Accountability is a critical component of the restorative justice process for offenders. It involves understanding the impact of their actions on victims and the community, and taking responsibility for those actions. This chapter explores the emotional journey of accountability, highlighting how restorative justice facilitates this process and its benefits for offenders.

The Concept of Accountability

Definition of Accountability

Accountability in the context of restorative justice means:

- Acknowledging Harm: Recognizing and admitting the harm caused to victims and the community.

- Taking Responsibility: Accepting responsibility for one's actions without making excuses or shifting blame.

- Making Amends: Committing to actions that repair the harm and contribute to personal and community healing.

Importance of Accountability for Offenders

Accountability is crucial for offenders because it:

- Promotes Self-Reflection: Encourages offenders to reflect on their behavior and its consequences.

- Fosters Empathy: Helps offenders develop empathy by understanding the victim's perspective.

- Facilitates Rehabilitation: Lays the foundation for personal growth and behavioral change.

Emotional Journey of Accountability

Initial Reactions: Guilt and Shame

Offenders often experience strong emotions when first confronted with the consequences of their actions:

- Guilt: A sense of guilt arises from recognizing that one's actions have caused harm. This emotion can be constructive, motivating the offender to make amends.

- Shame: Shame involves feeling humiliated or disgraced by one's actions. While potentially debilitating, when managed constructively, it can lead to positive change.

Confronting the Impact

Restorative justice processes help offenders confront the impact of their actions:

- Victim-Offender Dialogue: Direct dialogue with victims allows offenders to hear firsthand how their actions have affected others, fostering empathy and understanding.

- Facilitated Reflection: Facilitators guide offenders through reflective exercises, helping them to internalize the consequences of their behavior.

Restorative Justice Processes Facilitating Accountability

Victim-Offender Mediation

Process:

- Preparation: Offenders are prepared for the mediation process through discussions about expectations, the importance of listening, and the value of taking responsibility.

- Facilitated Dialogue: During mediation, offenders engage in a structured conversation with victims, acknowledging harm and discussing ways to make amends.

Benefits:

- Empathy Development: Direct interaction with victims fosters empathy and a deeper understanding of the impact of their actions.

- Personal Responsibility: The process encourages offenders to take personal responsibility, which is essential for genuine remorse and rehabilitation.

Restorative Circles

Process:

- Inclusive Participation: Offenders participate in restorative circles alongside victims and community members, engaging in open dialogue about the crime and its consequences.

- Collective Decision-Making: Participants collaboratively develop plans for reparation and support, with offenders taking an active role in proposing and committing to these actions.

Benefits:

- Shared Accountability: The inclusive nature of restorative circles promotes a sense of shared accountability and responsibility.

- Constructive Support: Community support enhances offenders' commitment to making amends and encourages positive behavioral change.

Benefits of Accountability

Emotional Relief

Taking responsibility can provide significant emotional relief for offenders:

- Alleviating Guilt: Acknowledging harm and making amends can alleviate feelings of guilt, replacing them with a sense of purpose and direction.

- Constructive Shame: Transforming shame into constructive actions helps offenders rebuild their self-esteem and self-worth.

Personal Growth and Rehabilitation

Accountability is a key driver of personal growth and rehabilitation:

- Self-Awareness: Reflecting on their actions increases offenders' self-awareness and understanding of their behavior patterns.

- Behavioral Change: Accepting responsibility motivates offenders to change their behavior and avoid future wrongdoing.

Restored Relationships

Accountability helps restore relationships with victims, families, and the community:

- Rebuilding Trust: Taking responsibility and making amends rebuilds trust and credibility with others.

- Community Reintegration: Accountability lays the groundwork for successful reintegration into the community, fostering acceptance and support.

Case Studies

Case Study 1: Youth Offender Program

Background:

- A restorative justice program was implemented for youth offenders involved in vandalism in an urban neighborhood.

Implementation:

- The program included victim-offender mediation sessions where offenders met with victims to discuss the impact of their actions.

- Offenders participated in community service projects as part of their reparation plans.

Outcomes:

- Offenders reported increased understanding of the harm caused and demonstrated genuine remorse.

- The program led to reduced recidivism rates and improved relationships between offenders and the community.

Analysis:

- The program effectively facilitated accountability by providing opportunities for reflection, empathy development, and constructive actions.

- The supportive environment of the mediation sessions enhanced offenders' commitment to making amends and changing their behavior.

Case Study 2: Restorative Circle for Assault

Background:

- A restorative justice program was introduced to address assault cases in a high school setting.

Implementation:

- The program involved restorative circles where offenders, victims, and community members engaged in open dialogue about the impact of the assault.

- Participants collaboratively developed reparation plans that included apologies, restitution, and community service.

Outcomes:

- Offenders demonstrated increased empathy and accountability, with a commitment to positive behavioral change.

- The process fostered a positive and inclusive school climate, with improved relationships among students.

Analysis:

- The restorative circles successfully facilitated accountability by promoting empathy, shared responsibility, and constructive actions.

- The active participation and social support provided by the community enhanced offenders' sense of responsibility and commitment to making amends.

Challenges and Considerations

Overcoming Denial and Resistance

- Emotional Resistance: Some offenders may initially resist taking responsibility due to fear, shame, or denial. Facilitators must create a safe and supportive environment that encourages openness and self-reflection.

- Building Trust: Establishing trust between facilitators, offenders, and victims is crucial for overcoming resistance and fostering genuine accountability.

Providing Ongoing Support

- Continuous Support: Providing ongoing emotional and psychological support to offenders throughout and after the restorative justice process is essential for sustained accountability and rehabilitation.

- Access to Resources: Ensuring that offenders have access to resources such as counseling, therapy, and support groups can enhance their personal growth and commitment to positive change.

Accountability is a fundamental aspect of restorative justice, encouraging offenders to understand the impact of their actions and take responsibility. By fostering empathy, promoting personal growth, and facilitating behavioral change, restorative justice processes help offenders achieve emotional relief, personal development, and restored relationships. Understanding the mechanisms and benefits of accountability is crucial for designing effective restorative justice programs that promote holistic recovery and well-being. As we continue to explore the emotional effects of restorative justice on offenders in this book, the insights gained from accountability will inform our broader discussion on creating a more just and compassionate society.

Reintegration: The Emotional Journey Towards Rejoining the Community

Reintegration is a crucial aspect of restorative justice, focusing on the emotional and social journey of offenders as they rejoin their communities. This chapter examines the emotional challenges and benefits of reintegration, highlighting how restorative justice processes support offenders in rebuilding their lives and relationships, and fostering a sense of belonging and acceptance within their communities.

The Concept of Reintegration

Definition of Reintegration

Reintegration refers to the process of re-establishing oneself within the community after having been involved in criminal behavior. It involves:

- Social Acceptance: Rebuilding trust and acceptance within the community.

- Personal Development: Addressing underlying issues and making positive behavioral changes.

- Support Systems: Establishing networks of support to facilitate successful reintegration.

Importance of Reintegration for Offenders

Reintegration is essential for offenders because it:

- Reduces Recidivism: Successful reintegration reduces the likelihood of reoffending by providing stability and support.

- Promotes Healing: Helps offenders heal from the psychological impacts of their actions and the consequences of their criminal behavior.

- Fosters Belonging: Encourages a sense of belonging and community, which is crucial for personal development and well-being.

Emotional Journey of Reintegration

Initial Challenges: Fear and Anxiety

Offenders often face significant emotional challenges during the initial stages of reintegration:

- Fear of Rejection: Fear of being rejected by the community and loved ones can create anxiety and hinder the reintegration process.

- Uncertainty: Uncertainty about their future and ability to change can lead to feelings of insecurity and self-doubt.

Overcoming Barriers

Restorative justice processes help offenders overcome barriers to reintegration:

- Building Trust: Restorative justice fosters trust by involving the community in the reintegration process, promoting transparency and open communication.

- Providing Support: Facilitators, community members, and support networks provide emotional and practical support to offenders, helping them navigate the challenges of reintegration.

Restorative Justice Processes Facilitating Reintegration

Community Restorative Circles

Process:

- Inclusive Participation: Restorative circles involve offenders, victims, and community members in a collective dialogue, focusing on the reintegration of offenders.

- Shared Support: Participants discuss the challenges and needs of offenders, developing plans for support and reparation.

Benefits:

- Community Acceptance: The inclusive nature of restorative circles promotes community acceptance and support for offenders.

- Collective Responsibility: The process fosters a sense of collective responsibility for the reintegration and well-being of offenders.

Family Group Conferencing

Process:

- Involving Families: Family group conferencing involves offenders, their families, and other supporters in a structured meeting to discuss reintegration.

- Collaborative Planning: Participants collaboratively develop plans for reparation and support, addressing the emotional and practical needs of offenders.

Benefits:

- Supportive Environment: The involvement of family members creates a supportive and empathetic environment, enhancing offenders' sense of belonging.

- Enhanced Support Networks: Family group conferencing strengthens support networks, providing ongoing emotional and practical support to offenders.

Benefits of Reintegration

Emotional Relief and Stability

Reintegration provides significant emotional relief and stability for offenders:

- Reduced Anxiety: Successful reintegration reduces feelings of fear and anxiety, providing a sense of security and stability.

- Emotional Support: Support from the community and family helps offenders manage emotional challenges and promotes emotional healing.

Personal Growth and Development

Reintegration fosters personal growth and development for offenders:

- Behavioral Change: Supportive reintegration processes encourage positive behavioral changes, helping offenders build new skills and habits.

- Self-Esteem: Successful reintegration enhances self-esteem and confidence, promoting a positive self-image and personal development.

Strengthened Relationships

Reintegration helps rebuild and strengthen relationships with victims, families, and the community:

- Rebuilding Trust: Taking responsibility and making amends rebuilds trust and credibility with others.

- Community Belonging: Successful reintegration fosters a sense of belonging and community, enhancing social cohesion and support.

Case Studies

Case Study 1: Community Restorative Circle for Theft

Background:

- A restorative justice program was implemented for offenders involved in theft in a rural community.

Implementation:

- The program included community restorative circles where offenders, victims, and community members engaged in dialogue about the impact of the theft and the offenders' reintegration.

- Participants developed reparation and support plans, focusing on rebuilding trust and providing emotional and practical support.

Outcomes:

- Offenders reported feeling accepted and supported by the community, with reduced anxiety and increased confidence in their ability to change.

- The program led to strengthened community relationships and reduced recidivism rates.

Analysis:

- The program effectively facilitated reintegration by providing opportunities for open dialogue, community support, and collective responsibility.

- The inclusive and supportive environment of the restorative circles enhanced offenders' sense of belonging and commitment to positive change.

Case Study 2: Family Group Conferencing for Assault

Background:

- A restorative justice program was introduced to address assault cases in an urban setting, focusing on the reintegration of offenders.

Implementation:

- The program involved family group conferencing, where offenders, their families, and other supporters engaged in structured meetings to discuss reintegration.

- Participants collaboratively developed reparation and support plans, addressing the emotional and practical needs of offenders.

Outcomes:

- Offenders demonstrated increased self-esteem and confidence, with a commitment to positive behavioral change.

- The process fostered stronger family relationships and enhanced support networks, promoting successful reintegration.

Analysis:

- The family group conferencing successfully facilitated reintegration by creating a supportive and empathetic environment.

- The involvement of family members and the development of comprehensive support plans enhanced offenders' sense of belonging and stability.

Challenges and Considerations

Addressing Stigma and Rejection

- Combating Stigma: Offenders may face stigma and rejection from the community. Facilitators must work to combat stigma and promote acceptance and understanding.

- Building Community Awareness: Raising awareness about the benefits of reintegration and restorative justice can help build community support and reduce stigma.

Providing Comprehensive Support

- Holistic Support: Providing comprehensive support, including emotional, psychological, and practical assistance, is essential for successful reintegration.

- Access to Resources: Ensuring that offenders have access to resources such as counseling, therapy, education, and employment opportunities can enhance their reintegration and personal development.

Reintegration is a crucial aspect of restorative justice, focusing on the emotional and social journey of offenders as they rejoin their communities. By providing opportunities for open dialogue, community support, and collective responsibility, restorative justice facilitates successful reintegration, promoting emotional relief, personal growth, and strengthened relationships. Understanding the mechanisms and benefits of reintegration is essential for designing effective restorative justice programs that promote holistic recovery and well-being. As we continue to explore the emotional effects of restorative justice on offenders in this book, the insights gained from reintegration will inform our broader discussion on creating a more just and compassionate society.

Collective Healing: The Community's Role in Supporting Both Victims and Offenders

Restorative justice is not only about addressing the needs of victims and offenders but also about engaging the community in the process of healing. Collective healing involves the entire community in supporting both victims and offenders, fostering a sense of shared responsibility and mutual support. This chapter explores the concept of collective healing, highlighting the community's role in restorative justice and the benefits of this approach.

Understanding Collective Healing

Definition of Collective Healing

Collective healing refers to the process by which a community comes together to address and heal from the harm caused by crime. It involves:

- Shared Responsibility: Recognizing that the well-being of individuals is interconnected with the well-being of the community.

- Mutual Support: Providing support to both victims and offenders to facilitate their healing and reintegration.

Importance of Collective Healing

Collective healing is essential because it:

- Promotes Social Cohesion: Strengthens the bonds between community members by fostering a sense of unity and mutual support.

- Addresses Root Causes: Tackles the underlying issues that contribute to crime, promoting long-term solutions and prevention.

- Enhances Community Resilience: Builds a resilient community capable of collectively addressing and overcoming challenges.

The Community's Role in Collective Healing

Supporting Victims

The community plays a crucial role in supporting victims through restorative justice processes:

- Validation and Empathy: Community members validate the experiences of victims by acknowledging the harm they have suffered and expressing empathy.

- Practical Support: Providing practical support such as assistance with daily needs, emotional support, and resources for recovery.

Supporting Offenders

The community also supports offenders, facilitating their rehabilitation and reintegration:

- Encouraging Accountability: Community members encourage offenders to take responsibility for their actions and make amends.

- Providing Opportunities: Offering opportunities for offenders to participate in community service, education, and employment, which are essential for successful reintegration.

Restorative Justice Processes Facilitating Collective Healing

Restorative Circles

Process:

- Inclusive Participation: Restorative circles involve victims, offenders, and community members in a collective dialogue, focusing on the impact of the crime and the needs of all participants.

- Collaborative Decision-Making: Participants collaboratively develop reparation plans and support strategies, ensuring that all voices are heard and respected.

Benefits:

- Empathy and Understanding: The inclusive nature of restorative circles fosters empathy and understanding among participants, promoting collective healing.

- Community Engagement: Engaging the community in the restorative process enhances social cohesion and collective responsibility.

Community Service Projects

Process:

- Offender Involvement: Offenders participate in community service projects as part of their reparation plans, contributing positively to the community.

- Community Support: Community members support these projects, working alongside offenders and providing mentorship and guidance.

Benefits:

- Restorative Actions: Community service projects allow offenders to make tangible contributions to the community, fostering a sense of accomplishment and belonging.

- Shared Goals: Collaborative projects build shared goals and foster a sense of unity and collective healing within the community.

Benefits of Collective Healing

Enhanced Social Cohesion

Collective healing enhances social cohesion by:

- Building Trust: Engaging in restorative justice processes builds trust among community members, fostering a sense of safety and solidarity.

- Promoting Unity: Collective healing promotes unity by addressing harm and working towards common goals, strengthening the fabric of the community.

Increased Collective Efficacy

Collective efficacy, or the community's belief in its ability to achieve shared goals, is enhanced through collective healing:

- Empowered Communities: Communities that engage in collective healing feel empowered to address and prevent future harm, increasing their resilience.

- Shared Responsibility: Collective efficacy is strengthened as community members recognize their shared responsibility in promoting justice and well-being.

Case Studies

Case Study 1: Restorative Circle for Vandalism

Background:

- A restorative justice program was implemented to address vandalism cases in a suburban community.

Implementation:

- The program included restorative circles where victims, offenders, and community members engaged in dialogue about the impact of the vandalism and the needs of all participants.

- Participants collaboratively developed reparation plans, including community service projects and support strategies for offenders.

Outcomes:

- The process fostered empathy and understanding among participants, promoting collective healing.

- Community service projects enhanced social cohesion and collective efficacy, with community members and offenders working together towards shared goals.

Analysis:

- The restorative circles effectively facilitated collective healing by promoting inclusive dialogue and collaborative decision-making.

- The involvement of the community in the restorative process enhanced social cohesion and collective responsibility.

Case Study 2: Community Service for Theft

Background:

- A restorative justice program was introduced to address theft cases in an urban neighborhood, focusing on collective healing and community involvement.

Implementation:

- The program involved community service projects where offenders worked alongside community members to repair the harm caused by theft.

- Community members provided mentorship and support, encouraging offenders to take responsibility and make positive contributions.

Outcomes:

- The community service projects fostered a sense of accomplishment and belonging among offenders, promoting their reintegration.

- The process strengthened relationships between community members and offenders, enhancing social cohesion and collective efficacy.

Analysis:

- The community service projects successfully facilitated collective healing by promoting restorative actions and shared goals.

- The involvement of the community in supporting offenders and fostering accountability enhanced social cohesion and collective responsibility.

Challenges and Considerations

Ensuring Inclusive Participation

- Diverse Representation: Ensuring diverse representation in restorative justice processes is crucial for fostering inclusive participation and collective healing.

- Overcoming Barriers: Addressing barriers to participation, such as stigma or lack of awareness, is essential for engaging the entire community in collective healing.

Providing Ongoing Support

- Continuous Engagement: Providing ongoing support and engagement opportunities for community members is essential for sustaining collective healing and social cohesion.

- Access to Resources: Ensuring that the community has access to resources and support networks can enhance their capacity for collective healing and resilience.

Collective healing is a fundamental aspect of restorative justice, involving the entire community in supporting both victims and offenders. By promoting shared responsibility, mutual support, and inclusive participation, restorative justice fosters social cohesion, collective efficacy, and long-term community resilience. Understanding the processes and benefits of collective healing is crucial for designing effective restorative justice programs that promote holistic recovery and well-being. As we continue to explore the emotional effects of restorative justice on community members in this book, the insights gained from collective healing will inform our broader discussion on creating a more just and compassionate society.

Strengthened Relationships: Building Stronger, More Empathetic Communities

One of the key outcomes of restorative justice is the strengthening of relationships within the community. By fostering empathy, understanding, and mutual respect, restorative justice builds stronger, more resilient communities. This chapter explores how restorative justice processes contribute to strengthened relationships, highlighting the benefits for both individuals and the broader community.

The Importance of Strengthened Relationships

Definition of Strengthened Relationships

Strengthened relationships refer to the development of deeper, more empathetic connections between community members. This involves:

- Empathy and Understanding: Fostering a genuine understanding of and empathy for others' experiences and perspectives.

- Mutual Respect: Building relationships based on mutual respect and recognition of each person's inherent dignity and worth.

- Collaboration and Support: Encouraging collaborative efforts and mutual support to address community issues and promote well-being.

Benefits of Strengthened Relationships

Strengthened relationships are crucial for the well-being of both individuals and communities:

- Enhanced Social Cohesion: Strong relationships foster social cohesion, creating a sense of unity and collective responsibility.

- Increased Resilience: Communities with strong relationships are better equipped to address and overcome challenges, enhancing overall resilience.

- Improved Well-Being: Positive relationships contribute to the emotional and psychological well-being of individuals, promoting a healthier and more supportive community.

Restorative Justice Processes Strengthening Relationships

Victim-Offender Mediation

Process:

- Facilitated Dialogue: Victim-offender mediation involves facilitated dialogue between victims and offenders, focusing on understanding the impact of the crime and developing a plan for reparation.

- Empathy Development: The process encourages empathy development by allowing both parties to share their experiences and perspectives.

Benefits:

- Restored Trust: The dialogue fosters trust and mutual understanding, helping to restore and strengthen relationships between victims and offenders.

- Collaborative Solutions: Collaborative problem-solving enhances the sense of partnership and mutual respect.

Restorative Circles

Process:

- Inclusive Participation: Restorative circles involve victims, offenders, and community members in a collective dialogue, focusing on the impact of the crime and the needs of all participants.

- Shared Decision-Making: Participants collaboratively develop reparation plans and support strategies, ensuring that all voices are heard and respected.

Benefits:

- Community Bonding: The inclusive nature of restorative circles fosters community bonding and collective responsibility.

- Empathy and Understanding: The process promotes empathy and understanding among participants, strengthening relationships and social cohesion.

Benefits of Strengthened Relationships

Enhanced Empathy and Understanding

Restorative justice processes enhance empathy and understanding by:

- Promoting Dialogue: Open dialogue fosters a genuine understanding of others' experiences and perspectives.

- Encouraging Reflection: Reflective practices encourage participants to consider the impact of their actions on others, fostering empathy and mutual respect.

Increased Social Cohesion

Strengthened relationships contribute to increased social cohesion by:

- Building Trust: Trust is built through collaborative problem-solving and mutual support, fostering a sense of unity and collective responsibility.

- Promoting Unity:

Addressing harm and working towards common goals promotes unity and strengthens the fabric of the community.

Case Studies

Case Study 1: Restorative Circle for Bullying

Background:

- A restorative justice program was implemented to address bullying cases in a high school setting.

Implementation:

- The program involved restorative circles where victims, offenders, and community members engaged in dialogue about the impact of the bullying and the needs of all participants.

- Participants collaboratively developed reparation plans, including apologies, restitution, and support strategies.

Outcomes:

- The process fostered empathy and understanding among participants, promoting stronger relationships and a positive school climate.

- Social cohesion was enhanced, with students reporting increased trust and mutual respect.

Analysis:

- The restorative circles effectively strengthened relationships by promoting inclusive dialogue and collaborative decision-making.

- The involvement of the community in the restorative process enhanced empathy, understanding, and social cohesion.

Case Study 2: Community Restorative Circle for Theft

Background:

- A restorative justice program was introduced to address theft cases in a rural community, focusing on strengthening relationships and community involvement.

Implementation:

- The program included community restorative circles where victims, offenders, and community members engaged in dialogue about the impact of the theft and the needs of all participants.

- Participants collaboratively developed reparation plans, focusing on rebuilding trust and providing support.

Outcomes:

- The process fostered empathy and understanding among participants, promoting stronger relationships and community bonding.

- Social cohesion and collective responsibility were enhanced, with community members reporting increased trust and mutual support.

Analysis:

- The restorative circles successfully strengthened relationships by promoting empathy, understanding, and collaborative problem-solving.

- The involvement of the community in the restorative process enhanced social cohesion and collective responsibility.

Challenges and Considerations

Ensuring Inclusive Participation

- Diverse Representation: Ensuring diverse representation in restorative justice processes is crucial for fostering inclusive participation and strengthened relationships.

- Overcoming Barriers: Addressing barriers to participation, such as stigma or lack of awareness, is essential for engaging the entire community in the process.

Providing Ongoing Support

- Continuous Engagement: Providing ongoing support and engagement opportunities for community members is essential for sustaining strengthened relationships and social cohesion.

- Access to Resources: Ensuring that the community has access to resources and support networks can enhance their capacity for building and maintaining strong relationships.

Strengthened relationships are a fundamental outcome of restorative justice, fostering empathy, understanding, and mutual respect within the community. By promoting inclusive dialogue, collaborative problem-solving, and mutual support, restorative justice builds stronger, more resilient communities. Understanding the processes and benefits of strengthened relationships is crucial for designing effective restorative justice programs that promote holistic recovery and well-being. As we continue to explore the emotional effects of restorative justice on community members in this book, the insights gained from strengthened relationships will inform our broader discussion on creating a more just and compassionate society.

CHAPTER 05

BENEFITS OF RESTORATIVE JUSTICE

Increased Empathy

Introduction

One of the most profound benefits of restorative justice is the development of empathy among participants. Empathy, the ability to understand and share the feelings of others, plays a crucial role in fostering understanding, healing, and positive behavioral change. This chapter explores how restorative justice practices foster empathy in both offenders and victims, and examines the long-term effects of increased empathy on behavior and relationships.

Empathy Development

Empathy in Restorative Justice

Restorative justice processes are designed to foster empathy by encouraging participants to understand and appreciate each other's experiences and emotions. This is achieved through several key mechanisms:

- Facilitated Dialogue: Structured conversations between victims and offenders provide a safe space for sharing personal stories and feelings, promoting mutual understanding.

- Active Listening: Participants are encouraged to actively listen to one another, which helps them to appreciate different perspectives and develop empathy.

- Reflective Practices: Reflective exercises and guided discussions help participants internalize the impact of their actions and the emotions of others.

Empathy Development in Offenders

Offenders often begin restorative justice processes with limited understanding of the impact of their actions. Restorative justice fosters empathy in offenders through:

- Victim Impact Statements: Hearing victims describe the personal impact of the crime helps offenders to see the human consequences of their actions, promoting empathy.

- Direct Interaction: Direct interaction with victims in a safe, facilitated environment allows offenders to engage with the emotional realities of their actions, breaking down barriers and fostering empathy.

- Reflective Dialogue: Facilitators guide offenders through reflective dialogues that encourage them to consider the emotions and perspectives of their victims, fostering deeper empathy and understanding.

Empathy Development in Victims

Victims also experience empathy development through restorative justice processes. This occurs through:

- Understanding Offenders' Perspectives: Hearing offenders' stories and the factors that contributed to their actions can help victims to develop empathy, even as they process their own emotions.

- Shared Humanity: Recognizing the shared humanity of both parties can help victims to move beyond anger and resentment, fostering a more empathetic outlook.

- Supportive Environment: The supportive environment of restorative justice processes allows victims to explore their own feelings and those of the offender in a safe space, promoting mutual empathy.

Long-term Effects of Increased Empathy

Positive Behavioral Change

Increased empathy has significant long-term effects on behavior, particularly for offenders:

- Reduced Recidivism: Offenders who develop empathy are less likely to reoffend, as they are more aware of the impact of their actions on others and motivated to avoid causing harm.

- Constructive Behavior: Empathy promotes constructive behavior and positive decision-making, as offenders seek to make amends and contribute positively to their communities.

- Personal Growth: The development of empathy fosters personal growth and self-awareness, helping offenders to build healthier relationships and lifestyles.

Strengthened Relationships

Increased empathy also leads to strengthened relationships within the community:

- Restored Trust: Empathy helps to restore trust between victims and offenders, as mutual understanding and respect are fostered through restorative justice processes.

- Enhanced Social Cohesion: Communities benefit from enhanced social cohesion as empathy promotes solidarity, mutual support, and collective responsibility.

- Positive Interactions: Empathy fosters positive interactions and relationships, reducing conflict and promoting a more compassionate and understanding community.

Case Studies

Case Study 1: Restorative Circle for Assault

Background:

- A restorative justice program was implemented to address assault cases in a high school setting.

Implementation:

- The program involved restorative circles where victims, offenders, and community members engaged in dialogue about the impact of the assault and the needs of all participants.

- Participants were guided through reflective exercises and active listening practices to foster empathy.

Outcomes:

- Offenders demonstrated increased empathy and understanding of the impact of their actions, leading to positive behavioral changes and reduced recidivism.

- Victims reported a greater sense of closure and empathy towards the offenders, contributing to their emotional healing.

Analysis:

- The restorative circles effectively fostered empathy through facilitated dialogue, active listening, and reflective practices.

- The increased empathy led to long-term positive effects on behavior and relationships, enhancing the overall school climate.

Case Study 2: Victim-Offender Mediation for Theft

Background:

- A restorative justice program was introduced to address theft cases in an urban neighborhood, focusing on empathy development and community involvement.

Implementation:

- The program included victim-offender mediation sessions where offenders met with victims to discuss the impact of the theft and develop reparation plans.

- Facilitators guided the dialogue, encouraging participants to share their feelings and perspectives.

Outcomes:

- Offenders developed a deeper understanding of the harm caused by their actions and demonstrated genuine remorse and empathy.

- Victims reported feeling heard and validated, with increased empathy towards the offenders.

Analysis:

- The victim-offender mediation sessions successfully fostered empathy by promoting open dialogue and mutual understanding.

- The long-term effects included reduced recidivism, improved relationships, and enhanced community cohesion.

Challenges and Considerations

Ensuring Effective Facilitation

- Trained Facilitators: Effective empathy development requires skilled facilitators who can guide the dialogue and reflective practices, ensuring that participants feel safe and supported.

- Creating Safe Spaces: Facilitators must create safe spaces where participants can openly share their feelings and perspectives without fear of judgment or retaliation.

Addressing Resistance

- Overcoming Resistance: Some participants may initially resist engaging in empathetic dialogue due to fear, shame, or anger. Facilitators must work to build trust and encourage openness.

- Building Trust: Establishing trust between facilitators, participants, and the community is crucial for fostering genuine empathy and understanding.

Empathy development is one of the most significant benefits of restorative justice, fostering mutual understanding, healing, and positive behavioral change. By promoting facilitated dialogue, active listening, and reflective practices, restorative justice processes help both offenders and victims to develop empathy, leading to long-term positive effects on behavior and relationships. Understanding the mechanisms and benefits of empathy development is crucial for designing effective restorative justice programs that promote holistic recovery and well-being. As we continue to explore the benefits of restorative justice in this book, the insights gained from empathy development will inform our broader discussion on creating a more just and compassionate society.

Healing and Reconciliation

Restorative justice offers a transformative approach to addressing the aftermath of crime, focusing on healing and reconciliation rather than mere punishment. This approach provides a platform for emotional recovery and the rebuilding of trust between individuals and within communities. This chapter explores the role of restorative justice in emotional and psychological healing, and how it helps rebuild trust, fostering a more cohesive and compassionate society.

Emotional Recovery

The Role of Restorative Justice in Emotional and Psychological Healing

Restorative justice places a strong emphasis on the emotional and psychological healing of all parties involved—victims, offenders, and the community. The processes and practices of restorative justice are designed to facilitate this healing in several key ways:

Providing a Safe Space for Expression

Restorative justice creates a safe and supportive environment where participants can express their emotions and experiences freely:

- Victim Impact Statements: Victims are given the opportunity to articulate the impact of the crime on their lives, sharing their pain, anger, and fears in a safe setting.

- Offender Testimonies: Offenders can express their remorse and acknowledge the harm they have caused, which is a crucial step in their emotional recovery.

Facilitated Dialogue and Mediation

The structured dialogue facilitated by trained mediators helps participants to process their emotions and move towards healing:

- Guided Conversations: Mediators guide the conversations to ensure that they remain respectful and productive, allowing participants to express their feelings without escalation.

- Mutual Understanding: Through dialogue, both victims and offenders can develop a deeper understanding of each other's perspectives, which is essential for emotional healing.

Emotional Support and Validation

Restorative justice processes provide emotional support and validation, which are critical for psychological healing:

- Community Support: Involving community members in the process helps provide a broader network of support, ensuring that participants do not feel isolated.

- Validation of Feelings: The acknowledgment of harm and the validation of participants' feelings by others contribute significantly to their emotional recovery.

Benefits of Emotional Recovery

Victims' Emotional Healing

For victims, the opportunity to express their emotions and receive validation can lead to significant emotional healing:

- Sense of Closure: Sharing their story and receiving acknowledgment helps victims achieve a sense of closure.

- Empowerment: Being heard and respected in the restorative justice process empowers victims, restoring their sense of agency.

Offenders' Emotional Healing

For offenders, acknowledging the harm they have caused and expressing remorse can be a powerful catalyst for emotional healing:

- Remorse and Accountability: Expressing genuine remorse and taking responsibility for their actions helps offenders to come to terms with their behavior and its consequences.

- Personal Growth: The process encourages personal reflection and growth, which are essential for emotional and psychological healing.

Rebuilding Trust

How Restorative Justice Helps Rebuild Trust Between Individuals and Within Communities

Trust is a fundamental component of social cohesion and community well-being. Restorative justice helps rebuild trust that has been damaged by crime through several key mechanisms:

Acknowledgment of Harm

One of the first steps in rebuilding trust is the acknowledgment of harm by the offender:

- Taking Responsibility: When offenders acknowledge their wrongdoing and the impact of their actions, it helps to restore the trust of the victims and the community.

- Genuine Apologies: A sincere apology from the offender can be a powerful gesture that initiates the rebuilding of trust.

Collaborative Problem-Solving

Restorative justice processes involve collaborative problem-solving, which fosters mutual respect and trust:

- Shared Decision-Making: Involving victims, offenders, and community members in the decision-making process ensures that all voices are heard and respected, fostering trust.

- Developing Reparation Plans: Collaborative development of reparation plans allows all parties to work together towards a common goal, building trust through cooperation.

Restorative Practices in Community

Restorative practices within the community contribute to the rebuilding of trust on a broader scale:

- Community Circles: Regular community circles and meetings provide a platform for ongoing dialogue and support, reinforcing trust and social bonds.

- Community Service: Offenders participating in community service as part of their reparation plan demonstrate their commitment to making amends, which helps to restore community trust.

Benefits of Rebuilding Trust

Individual Trust Restoration

For victims and offenders, the restoration of trust has profound personal benefits:

- Healing Relationships: Restorative justice can heal damaged relationships by fostering mutual understanding and respect.

- Enhanced Well-Being: Restoring trust contributes to the emotional and psychological well-being of both victims and offenders.

Community Trust Restoration

For the broader community, rebuilding trust enhances social cohesion and resilience:

- Stronger Social Bonds: Communities with high levels of trust are more cohesive and supportive, leading to stronger social bonds.

- Increased Collective Efficacy: Trust within the community enhances collective efficacy, enabling the community to effectively address and prevent future conflicts and harms.

Case Studies

Case Study 1: Restorative Circle for Community Theft

Background:

- A restorative justice program was implemented to address a series of thefts in a small community.

Implementation:

- The program involved restorative circles where victims, offenders, and community members engaged in dialogue about the impact of the thefts and the needs of all participants.

- Participants collaboratively developed reparation plans and support strategies.

Outcomes:

- The process fostered empathy, understanding, and mutual respect among participants, promoting emotional recovery and trust.

- Community service projects were initiated as part of the reparation plans, enhancing community trust and cohesion.

Analysis:

- The restorative circles effectively facilitated emotional healing and trust rebuilding by promoting inclusive dialogue and collaborative problem-solving.

- The involvement of the community in the restorative process enhanced social cohesion and collective efficacy.

Case Study 2: Victim-Offender Mediation for Assault

Background:

- A restorative justice program was introduced to address assault cases in an urban neighborhood, focusing on emotional recovery and trust rebuilding.

Implementation:

- The program included victim-offender mediation sessions where offenders met with victims to discuss the impact of the assault and develop reparation plans.

- Facilitators guided the dialogue, encouraging participants to share their feelings and perspectives.

Outcomes:

- Victims reported significant emotional healing, with a sense of closure and empowerment.

- Offenders demonstrated genuine remorse and commitment to making amends, which helped rebuild trust with victims and the community.

Analysis:

- The victim-offender mediation sessions successfully facilitated emotional healing and trust rebuilding by promoting open dialogue and mutual respect.

- The long-term effects included improved relationships, enhanced community cohesion, and reduced recidivism.

Challenges and Considerations

Ensuring Effective Facilitation

- Trained Facilitators: Effective emotional recovery and trust rebuilding require skilled facilitators who can guide the dialogue and reflective practices, ensuring that participants feel safe and supported.

- Creating Safe Spaces: Facilitators must create safe spaces where participants can openly share their feelings and perspectives without fear of judgment or retaliation.

Addressing Resistance

- Overcoming Resistance: Some participants may initially resist engaging in empathetic dialogue due to fear, shame, or anger. Facilitators must work to build trust and encourage openness.

- Building Trust: Establishing trust between facilitators, participants, and the community is crucial for fostering genuine empathy and understanding.

Restorative justice provides a powerful platform for healing and reconciliation, promoting emotional recovery and the rebuilding of trust. By facilitating safe and supportive dialogue, validating feelings, and fostering mutual respect, restorative justice helps both victims and offenders to heal emotionally and rebuild trust. Understanding the mechanisms and benefits of emotional recovery and trust rebuilding is crucial for designing effective restorative justice programs that promote holistic recovery and well-being. As we continue to explore the benefits of restorative justice in this book, the insights gained from healing and reconciliation will inform our broader discussion on creating a more just and compassionate society.

Reduced Recidivism

Behavioral Changes: How Restorative Justice Influences Future Behavior

One of the most significant benefits of restorative justice is its ability to reduce recidivism, or the likelihood of reoffending. By addressing the underlying causes of criminal behavior and fostering personal accountability and empathy, restorative justice helps offenders make positive behavioral changes. This chapter explores the mechanisms through which restorative justice influences future behavior and contributes to lower rates of recidivism.

Mechanisms of Behavioral Change

Accountability and Responsibility

Restorative justice processes emphasize accountability, encouraging offenders to take responsibility for their actions:

- Acknowledgment of Harm: Offenders are required to acknowledge the harm they have caused to victims and the community, which fosters a sense of responsibility.

- Personal Responsibility: Taking responsibility for their actions motivates offenders to change their behavior and avoid causing harm in the future.

Empathy Development

Empathy development is a key component of restorative justice that influences behavior:

- Understanding Impact: Through direct dialogue with victims, offenders develop a deeper understanding of the emotional and psychological impact of their actions, fostering empathy.

- Motivation to Change: Empathy motivates offenders to change their behavior to avoid causing further harm and to make amends for past actions.

Reflective Practices

Restorative justice incorporates reflective practices that encourage personal growth and behavioral change:

- Self-Reflection: Offenders engage in self-reflection, considering the reasons for their behavior and the consequences of their actions.

- Guided Reflection: Facilitators guide offenders through reflective exercises that promote insight and self-awareness, essential for lasting behavioral change.

Processes Facilitating Behavioral Change

Victim-Offender Mediation

Process:

- Preparation: Facilitators prepare offenders for mediation by discussing the importance of taking responsibility and understanding the victim's perspective.

- Facilitated Dialogue: During mediation, offenders engage in structured dialogue with victims, acknowledging harm and discussing ways to make amends.

Benefits:

- Enhanced Empathy: Direct interaction with victims fosters empathy and a deeper understanding of the impact of their actions.

- Personal Accountability: The process encourages offenders to take personal responsibility, which is crucial for genuine remorse and behavioral change.

Restorative Circles

Process:

- Inclusive Participation: Restorative circles involve offenders, victims, and community members in a collective dialogue, focusing on the impact of the crime and the needs of all participants.

- Collaborative Decision-Making: Participants collaboratively develop reparation plans and support strategies, ensuring that all voices are heard and respected.

Benefits:

- Community Support: The inclusive nature of restorative circles provides a support system that encourages positive behavioral change.

- Shared Responsibility: The process fosters a sense of shared responsibility and accountability, reinforcing the motivation to avoid future offending.

Case Studies

Case Study 1: Victim-Offender Mediation for Burglary

Background:

- A restorative justice program was implemented for offenders involved in burglary in an urban community.

Implementation:

- The program included victim-offender mediation sessions where offenders met with victims to discuss the impact of the burglary and develop reparation plans.

- Facilitators guided the dialogue, encouraging empathy development and personal accountability.

Outcomes:

- Offenders demonstrated increased empathy and understanding of the harm caused by their actions, leading to positive behavioral changes.

- The program led to reduced recidivism rates, with offenders reporting a commitment to avoiding future offending.

Analysis:

- The victim-offender mediation sessions effectively facilitated behavioral change by promoting empathy, personal responsibility, and reflective practices.

- The inclusive and supportive environment of the mediation sessions enhanced offenders' motivation to change their behavior and make amends.

Case Study 2: Restorative Circle for Assault

Background:

- A restorative justice program was introduced to address assault cases in a high school setting.

Implementation:

- The program involved restorative circles where offenders, victims, and community members engaged in dialogue about the impact of the assault and the needs of all participants.

- Participants collaboratively developed reparation plans and support strategies, focusing on behavioral change and community support.

Outcomes:

- Offenders demonstrated increased empathy and accountability, with a commitment to positive behavioral change.

- The process fostered a positive and inclusive school climate, with improved relationships and reduced incidents of reoffending.

Analysis:

- The restorative circles successfully facilitated behavioral change by promoting empathy, shared responsibility, and collaborative decision-making.

- The active participation and social support provided by the community enhanced offenders' motivation to change their behavior and avoid future offending.

Benefits of Behavioral Change

Personal Growth and Development

Behavioral change through restorative justice promotes personal growth and development for offenders:

- Self-Awareness: Reflective practices increase self-awareness, helping offenders understand the root causes of their behavior and the impact on others.

- Positive Decision-Making: Offenders develop the skills and motivation to make positive decisions, reducing the likelihood of reoffending.

Enhanced Relationships

Behavioral change also leads to enhanced relationships between offenders, victims, and the community:

- Restored Trust: Taking responsibility and making amends helps to restore trust and credibility with victims and the community.

- Stronger Social Bonds: Positive behavioral change fosters stronger social bonds and a sense of belonging within the community.

Challenges and Considerations

Addressing Resistance to Change

- Emotional Resistance: Some offenders may initially resist engaging in empathetic dialogue and taking responsibility for their actions. Facilitators must work to build trust and encourage openness.

- Building Trust: Establishing trust between facilitators, offenders, and victims is crucial for fostering genuine behavioral change.

Providing Ongoing Support

- Continuous Support: Providing ongoing emotional and practical support to offenders throughout and after the restorative justice process is essential for sustained behavioral change.

- Access to Resources: Ensuring that offenders have access to resources such as counseling, therapy, education, and employment opportunities can enhance their personal growth and commitment to positive change.

Behavioral change is a fundamental benefit of restorative justice, contributing to reduced recidivism and promoting personal growth and development. By fostering empathy, personal responsibility, and reflective practices, restorative justice helps offenders to understand the impact of their actions and make positive behavioral changes. Understanding the mechanisms and benefits of behavioral change is crucial for designing effective restorative justice programs that promote holistic recovery and well-being. As we continue to explore the benefits of restorative justice in this book, the insights gained from behavioral change will inform our broader discussion on creating a more just and compassionate society.

Supporting Data: Research and Statistics Supporting the Reduction in Recidivism

Restorative justice has gained attention not only for its holistic approach to crime and conflict resolution but also for its effectiveness in reducing recidivism rates. This chapter presents supporting data from various research studies and statistical analyses that highlight how restorative justice programs contribute to lowering reoffending rates among participants.

Overview of Research on Recidivism Reduction

Defining Recidivism

Recidivism generally refers to the tendency of previously convicted individuals to reoffend. It is commonly measured through:

- Re-Arrest Rates: The frequency at which former offenders are re-arrested.

- Re-Conviction Rates: The rate at which former offenders are convicted of new crimes.

- Reincarceration Rates: The frequency at which former offenders are sentenced to prison again.

Key Studies and Findings

Meta-Analyses and Systematic Reviews

Meta-Analysis by Latimer, Dowden, and Muise (2005):

- Scope: This comprehensive meta-analysis reviewed 35 studies on restorative justice programs.

- Findings: The analysis revealed a significant reduction in recidivism rates among participants in restorative justice programs compared to those in traditional criminal justice systems. On average, restorative justice participants were 14% less likely to reoffend.

Systematic Review by Sherman and Strang (2007):

- Scope: This review included various restorative justice programs, such as victim-offender mediation and family group conferencing.

- Findings: The authors found consistent evidence that restorative justice programs reduced reoffending rates. Specifically, recidivism was reduced by an average of 27% compared to control groups receiving traditional sanctions.

Individual Studies

Study on Youth Offenders by Nugent, Umbreit, Wiinamaki, and Paddock (2001):

- Scope: This study focused on youth offenders participating in victim-offender mediation programs.

- Findings: The results showed a 32% reduction in recidivism rates among youth offenders who participated in restorative justice programs compared to those who did not.

Research by Bonta, Jesseman, Rugge, and Cormier (2006):

- Scope: This study examined the impact of restorative justice on adult offenders.

- Findings: The research indicated that adult offenders who participated in restorative justice programs had recidivism rates 11% lower than those processed through traditional criminal justice systems.

Evaluation of the Winnipeg Restorative Justice Program (2016):

- Scope: This program targeted a diverse group of offenders, including both youth and adults.

- Findings: The evaluation reported a 25% reduction in reoffending rates among participants. Additionally, the program noted improvements in participant accountability and victim satisfaction.

Statistical Highlights

National and International Statistics

United States:

- Bureau of Justice Statistics (BJS) Report (2016): The BJS reported that restorative justice programs implemented in various states showed recidivism reductions ranging from 10% to 20% compared to traditional corrections.

United Kingdom:

- Ministry of Justice (2015): The UK Ministry of Justice published findings showing that restorative justice conferencing reduced the frequency of reoffending by 14% on average.

Canada:

- Correctional Service Canada (2018): Restorative justice programs within Canadian correctional facilities reported a 15% reduction in recidivism rates among participants.

Australia:

- Australian Institute of Criminology (2013): A study found that restorative justice conferencing led to a 15-20% decrease in reoffending rates among juvenile offenders.

Case Studies and Program Evaluations

Case Study: New Zealand Family Group Conferencing

Background:

- New Zealand implemented family group conferencing as part of its juvenile justice system in the late 1980s.

Findings:

- A long-term evaluation indicated that participants in family group conferencing had significantly lower recidivism rates compared to those processed through traditional juvenile courts. Specifically, the reoffending rate was reduced by approximately 25%.

Case Study: Victim-Offender Mediation in Minnesota

Background:

- Minnesota's restorative justice programs, particularly victim-offender mediation, have been extensively evaluated.

Findings:

- Research demonstrated that participants in victim-offender mediation had a recidivism rate that was 34% lower than that of non-participants. Additionally, high levels of victim satisfaction and offender accountability were reported.

Mechanisms Behind Reduced Recidivism

Enhanced Empathy and Responsibility

- Empathy Development: Restorative justice processes foster empathy in offenders by encouraging them to understand and acknowledge the impact of their actions on victims.

- Personal Responsibility: The requirement to take responsibility and make amends helps offenders internalize the consequences of their actions, promoting behavioral change.

Community Support and Reintegration

- Community Involvement: The active involvement of community members in restorative justice processes provides a support network that facilitates the reintegration of offenders.

- Reparation Plans: Collaborative development of reparation plans ensures that offenders actively contribute to repairing the harm, which reinforces positive behaviors.

Psychological and Emotional Benefits

Emotional Healing: Addressing the emotional and psychological needs of both victims and offenders helps reduce the emotional drivers of criminal behavior.

- Sense of Closure: Providing a sense of closure for victims and accountability for offenders helps break the cycle of reoffending.

Challenges and Considerations

Ensuring Program Integrity

- Training and Resources: Successful implementation of restorative justice programs requires well-trained facilitators and adequate resources to support participants.

- Consistency and Monitoring: Ongoing monitoring and evaluation are necessary to ensure that programs are consistently delivering positive outcomes and reducing recidivism.

Addressing Diverse Needs

- Individualized Approaches: Restorative justice programs must be tailored to address the diverse needs of participants, including cultural, emotional, and social factors.

- Holistic Support: Providing holistic support that includes counseling, education, and employment opportunities can enhance the effectiveness of restorative justice in reducing recidivism.

The data supporting the effectiveness of restorative justice in reducing recidivism is compelling. Research studies and statistical analyses consistently show that restorative justice programs lead to significant reductions in reoffending rates among participants. By fostering empathy, personal responsibility, and community support, restorative justice facilitates positive behavioral changes that contribute to long-term reductions in recidivism. Understanding the supporting data is crucial for advocating the broader adoption and implementation of restorative justice programs as a viable alternative to traditional criminal justice systems. As we continue to explore the benefits of restorative justice in this book, the insights gained from supporting data will inform our broader discussion on creating a more just and compassionate society.

219

CHAPTER 06

RISKS AND CHALLENGES

Emotional Risks for Victims

Re-traumatization: The Potential for Victims to Relive Traumatic Experiences

Introduction

While restorative justice offers significant benefits, it also carries inherent risks, particularly for victims. One of the most pressing concerns is the potential for re-traumatization—where victims may relive traumatic experiences during the restorative process. This chapter explores the concept of re-traumatization, its causes, and how restorative justice processes can be structured to minimize this risk.

Understanding Re-traumatization

Definition of Re-traumatization

Re-traumatization occurs when individuals are exposed to reminders of their trauma, causing them to re-experience the emotional and psychological distress associated with the original event. In the context of restorative justice, re-traumatization can happen when victims are asked to recount their experiences or confront offenders.

Symptoms of Re-traumatization

Victims experiencing re-traumatization may exhibit a range of symptoms, including:

- Emotional Distress: Intense feelings of fear, anger, sadness, or helplessness.

- Physical Symptoms: Somatic complaints such as headaches, nausea, or rapid heartbeat.

- Psychological Symptoms: Flashbacks, nightmares, or intrusive thoughts related to the traumatic event.

- Behavioral Changes: Withdrawal from social activities, changes in sleep patterns, or increased substance use.

Causes of Re-traumatization in Restorative Justice

Direct Confrontation with Offenders

One of the primary causes of re-traumatization in restorative justice is the direct confrontation between victims and offenders:

- Emotional Triggers: Seeing or hearing the offender can trigger memories of the traumatic event, leading to intense emotional reactions.

- Power Imbalances: The presence of the offender may reinforce feelings of vulnerability and powerlessness, exacerbating the victim's distress.

Recounting Traumatic Experiences

The process of sharing one's story can be therapeutic but also carries the risk of re-traumatization:

- Emotional Overload: Recounting the details of the traumatic event can overwhelm victims, causing them to relive the distressing emotions associated with the experience.

- Lack of Readiness: Victims who are not emotionally prepared to discuss their trauma may experience heightened distress and re-traumatization.

Minimizing the Risk of Re-traumatization

Comprehensive Preparation

Proper preparation of victims before engaging in restorative justice processes is crucial to minimize the risk of re-traumatization:

- Emotional Readiness Assessments: Facilitators should assess the emotional readiness of victims, ensuring they are prepared to participate without undue distress.

- Pre-Session Support: Providing counseling and support prior to the restorative justice sessions can help victims process their emotions and prepare for the interaction.

Skilled Facilitation

Skilled facilitators play a vital role in managing the restorative justice process to prevent re-traumatization:

- Creating Safe Spaces: Facilitators must ensure that the environment is safe and supportive, allowing victims to express themselves without fear of judgment or retaliation.

- Guiding Dialogue: Facilitators should guide the dialogue carefully, ensuring that discussions do not become overly intense or distressing for victims.

Flexibility and Choice

Providing victims with flexibility and choice throughout the restorative justice process can help mitigate the risk of re-traumatization:

- Voluntary Participation: Participation in restorative justice should always be voluntary, with victims having the option to withdraw at any time if they feel uncomfortable.

- Control Over Engagement: Victims should have control over how and when they engage with the process, including the option to use written statements or proxies instead of direct confrontation.

Support Systems

Psychological Support

Ongoing psychological support is essential for victims participating in restorative justice:

- Access to Counseling: Ensuring that victims have access to counseling and mental health services can help them process their emotions and cope with potential re-traumatization.

- Support Groups: Participation in support groups with other victims can provide a sense of solidarity and shared understanding, reducing feelings of isolation.

Community and Family Support

Involving the community and family in the restorative justice process can provide additional layers of support for victims:

- Family Involvement: Family members can offer emotional support and reassurance, helping victims feel safer and more secure.

- Community Engagement: Community members can provide practical support and advocacy, reinforcing the victim's sense of belonging and support.

Case Studies

Case Study 1: Restorative Circle for Domestic Violence

Background:

- A restorative justice program was implemented to address domestic violence cases, focusing on providing support for victims and ensuring their emotional safety.

Implementation:

- The program included comprehensive preparation for victims, with emotional readiness assessments and pre-session counseling.

- Skilled facilitators guided the restorative circles, ensuring that the dialogue remained supportive and non-triggering.

Outcomes:

- Victims reported feeling supported and validated throughout the process, with minimal instances of re-traumatization.

- The structured and supportive environment helped victims to engage in the process without experiencing overwhelming distress.

Analysis:

- The program effectively minimized the risk of re-traumatization by providing thorough preparation and skilled facilitation.

- The involvement of family and community members provided additional layers of support, enhancing the emotional safety of victims.

Case Study 2: Victim-Offender Mediation for Sexual Assault

Background:

- A restorative justice program was introduced to address sexual assault cases, with a strong focus on preventing re-traumatization for victims.

Implementation:

- The program offered victims the choice of using written statements or proxies instead of direct confrontation with offenders.

- Ongoing psychological support was provided, including access to counseling and participation in support groups.

Outcomes:

- Victims who opted for written statements or proxies reported feeling more in control and less distressed during the process.

- The availability of psychological support helped victims to process their emotions and cope with the potential for re-traumatization.

Analysis:

- The program successfully mitigated the risk of re-traumatization by offering flexible engagement options and robust psychological support.

- The emphasis on victim choice and control contributed to a safer and more supportive restorative justice experience.

Challenges and Considerations

Balancing Accountability and Emotional Safety

- Victim Needs: Ensuring that the needs and emotional safety of victims are prioritized, while still holding offenders accountable, is a delicate balance that requires careful management.

- Tailored Approaches: Restorative justice processes should be tailored to the individual needs and circumstances of each victim, recognizing that there is no one-size-fits-all approach.

Continuous Monitoring and Support

- Ongoing Assessment: Continuous assessment of victims' emotional states throughout the restorative justice process is essential to identify and address any signs of re-traumatization promptly.

- Long-Term Support: Providing long-term support and follow-up services can help victims to continue their healing journey and mitigate any delayed effects of re-traumatization.

Conclusion

Re-traumatization is a significant risk in restorative justice processes, particularly for victims. However, with comprehensive preparation, skilled facilitation, and robust support systems, this risk can be minimized. Understanding the potential for re-traumatization and implementing strategies to mitigate it is crucial for ensuring that restorative justice processes are safe, supportive, and beneficial for all participants. As we continue to explore the risks and challenges of restorative justice in this book, the insights gained from addressing re-traumatization will inform our broader discussion on creating effective and compassionate restorative justice programs.

Expectations Management: Ensuring That Victims Have Realistic Expectations of the Process

Managing expectations is a critical component of restorative justice, particularly for victims. Unrealistic expectations can lead to dissatisfaction, disappointment, and even re-traumatization. Ensuring that victims have a clear, realistic understanding of the restorative justice process helps to create a supportive and effective environment for healing and resolution. This chapter explores strategies for managing expectations, the importance of clear communication, and the role of facilitators in guiding victims through the process.

The Importance of Managing Expectations

Preventing Disappointment and Frustration

Unrealistic expectations can lead to disappointment and frustration for victims:

- Expecting Complete Resolution: Victims may expect that all their emotional and psychological needs will be fully resolved through the restorative justice process, which is often not the case.

- Immediate Results: Some victims may expect immediate changes or reparations, while restorative justice typically involves ongoing processes and gradual improvements.

Ensuring Emotional Safety

Managing expectations is crucial for maintaining the emotional safety of victims:

- Avoiding Re-Traumatization: Clear communication about what to expect helps prevent re-traumatization by reducing the likelihood of unexpected or distressing experiences.

- Building Trust: Honest and transparent discussions about the process help to build trust between victims and facilitators, fostering a safe and supportive environment.

Strategies for Managing Expectations

Clear Communication

Effective communication is essential for setting realistic expectations:

- Detailed Explanations: Provide victims with detailed explanations of the restorative justice process, including the steps involved, potential outcomes, and timeframes.

- Honesty and Transparency: Be honest about the limitations of the process and the potential challenges, ensuring that victims have a balanced understanding of what to expect.

Setting Realistic Goals

Helping victims set realistic goals can guide their expectations and enhance their experience:

- Specific Objectives: Encourage victims to set specific, achievable objectives for their participation in the restorative justice process.

- Incremental Progress: Emphasize the importance of incremental progress and small victories, rather than expecting complete resolution or immediate results.

Providing Support and Resources

Offering support and resources helps victims feel prepared and informed:

- Pre-Session Counseling: Provide counseling and support sessions before restorative justice meetings to help victims process their emotions and clarify their expectations.

- Educational Materials: Offer educational materials, such as brochures or videos, that outline the restorative justice process and provide examples of typical outcomes.

Role of Facilitators in Managing Expectations

Initial Assessments

Facilitators play a crucial role in managing expectations through initial assessments:

- Emotional Readiness: Assess the emotional readiness of victims to participate in the restorative justice process, ensuring they are prepared for the experience.

- Expectations Discussion: Discuss the victim's expectations in detail, addressing any unrealistic or overly optimistic views and providing a more balanced perspective.

Ongoing Guidance

Continuous guidance from facilitators helps maintain realistic expectations:

- Regular Check-Ins: Conduct regular check-ins with victims throughout the process to reassess their expectations and address any emerging concerns or misconceptions.

- Adjusting Expectations: Help victims adjust their expectations as needed, based on their experiences and the progress of the restorative justice process.

Case Studies

Case Study 1: Victim-Offender Mediation for Theft

Background:

- A restorative justice program was implemented to address theft cases in a suburban community.

Implementation:

- Facilitators conducted initial assessments with victims to discuss their expectations and provide detailed explanations of the mediation process.

- Pre-session counseling and educational materials were offered to help victims prepare for the mediation sessions.

Outcomes:

- Victims reported feeling well-prepared and informed, with realistic expectations of the mediation process.

- The mediation sessions resulted in meaningful dialogue and reparation plans, with victims expressing satisfaction with the outcomes.

Analysis:

- The program successfully managed expectations by providing clear communication, setting realistic goals, and offering support and resources.

- The role of facilitators in guiding victims through the process and maintaining regular check-ins was crucial for ensuring a positive experience.

Case Study 2: Restorative Circle for Assault

Background:

- A restorative justice program was introduced to address assault cases in an urban neighborhood, with a focus on managing victim expectations.

Implementation:

- Facilitators held initial meetings with victims to discuss the restorative circle process, potential outcomes, and the importance of setting realistic goals.

- Victims received ongoing support and regular check-ins throughout the process to reassess their expectations and address any concerns.

Outcomes:

- Victims felt supported and informed, with a clear understanding of the restorative circle process and realistic expectations.

- The restorative circles facilitated constructive dialogue and reparation plans, leading to positive outcomes for both victims and offenders.

Analysis:

- The program effectively managed expectations by emphasizing the importance of clear communication, realistic goals, and ongoing support.

- The involvement of facilitators in providing continuous guidance and reassessment was key to ensuring a positive experience for victims.

Challenges and Considerations

Balancing Hope and Realism

- Encouraging Hope: While it is important to set realistic expectations, facilitators must also encourage hope and optimism, ensuring that victims feel positive about the potential for healing and resolution.

- Avoiding Pessimism: Striking a balance between realism and hope is crucial to prevent victims from feeling discouraged or pessimistic about the restorative justice process.

Addressing Diverse Needs

- Individualized Approaches: Victims have diverse needs and expectations, requiring individualized approaches to managing expectations.

- Cultural Sensitivity: Facilitators must be culturally sensitive, recognizing that cultural factors can influence victims' expectations and experiences of restorative justice.

Conclusion

Managing expectations is a critical aspect of restorative justice, ensuring that victims have a clear, realistic understanding of the process and potential outcomes. Through clear communication, setting realistic goals, and providing ongoing support and resources, facilitators can help victims feel prepared, informed, and emotionally safe. Understanding the importance of expectations management and implementing effective strategies is crucial for creating a supportive and effective restorative justice environment. As we continue to explore the risks and challenges of restorative justice in this book, the insights gained from managing expectations will inform our broader discussion on creating effective and compassionate restorative justice programs.

Emotional Risks for Offenders

Shame and Guilt: Navigating Intense Emotions That Can Arise During the Process

Introduction

While restorative justice offers numerous benefits, it also presents significant emotional challenges for offenders.

Among the most intense emotions that offenders may face are shame and guilt. These feelings, while integral to the process of accountability and rehabilitation, can be overwhelming and difficult to navigate. This chapter explores the nature of shame and guilt, their impacts on offenders, and strategies for managing these emotions within restorative justice frameworks.

Understanding Shame and Guilt

Definitions and Differences

Shame and guilt, though often used interchangeably, are distinct emotions with different implications for behavior and self-perception:

- Shame: A feeling of humiliation or distress caused by the awareness of wrong or foolish behavior. It is often associated with a sense of being fundamentally flawed or unworthy.

- Guilt: A feeling of responsibility or remorse for some offense, crime, wrong, etc., whether real or imagined. Guilt is more focused on the specific behavior and its consequences.

The Role of Shame and Guilt in Restorative Justice

Shame and guilt play crucial roles in the restorative justice process:

- Accountability: These emotions help offenders acknowledge the harm caused by their actions and take responsibility.

- Motivation for Change: Guilt can motivate offenders to make amends and avoid future wrongdoing, while shame can push them to seek personal growth and transformation.

The Impact of Shame and Guilt on Offenders

Emotional and Psychological Effects

The emotional and psychological impacts of shame and guilt on offenders can be profound:

- Shame: Can lead to feelings of worthlessness, isolation, and depression. It may also cause defensive behaviors, such as denial or aggression.

- Guilt: While potentially constructive, excessive guilt can result in anxiety, self-criticism, and diminished self-esteem.

Behavioral Consequences

Shame and guilt can influence offenders' behavior in various ways:

- Constructive Outcomes: Properly managed, these emotions can lead to positive behavioral changes, empathy, and efforts to make amends.

- Destructive Outcomes: If unaddressed, shame and guilt can contribute to recidivism, substance abuse, and other harmful behaviors as coping mechanisms.

Navigating Shame and Guilt in Restorative Justice

Facilitator's Role in Managing Emotions

Facilitators play a critical role in helping offenders navigate shame and guilt:

- Creating a Safe Environment: Establishing a supportive and non-judgmental environment where offenders can express their emotions without fear of condemnation.

- Guided Reflection: Encouraging offenders to reflect on their actions and the emotions they elicit in a constructive manner.

Therapeutic Interventions

Therapeutic interventions can assist offenders in managing their shame and guilt:

- Counseling and Therapy: Providing access to professional counseling and therapy to help offenders process their emotions and develop coping strategies.

- Support Groups: Facilitating support groups where offenders can share their experiences and feelings with others who understand their situation.

Restorative Practices

Incorporating specific restorative practices can help address shame and guilt:

- Victim-Offender Dialogue: Structured dialogues that allow offenders to express remorse and understand the impact of their actions, fostering empathy and reducing shame.

- Reparation and Amends: Encouraging offenders to make amends through tangible actions, which can alleviate guilt and promote a sense of redemption.

Benefits of Addressing Shame and Guilt

Personal Growth and Rehabilitation

Effectively managing shame and guilt can lead to significant personal growth and rehabilitation:

- Enhanced Self-Awareness: Offenders gain a deeper understanding of their behavior and its impact, which is essential for personal transformation.

- Positive Behavioral Change: Addressing these emotions constructively can motivate offenders to change their behavior and avoid future wrongdoing.

Improved Relationships

Addressing shame and guilt can improve relationships between offenders, victims, and the community:

- Restored Trust: Taking responsibility and making amends can help rebuild trust with victims and the community.

- Enhanced Empathy: Understanding and addressing their emotions can make offenders more empathetic, improving their relationships with others.

Case Studies

Case Study 1: Victim-Offender Mediation for Assault

Background:

- A restorative justice program was implemented to address assault cases, focusing on helping offenders navigate shame and guilt.

Implementation:

- Facilitators provided pre-session counseling to offenders, helping them understand and prepare for the emotional challenges of the process.

- During mediation, offenders were encouraged to express their remorse and discuss the impact of their actions with victims in a supportive environment.

Outcomes:

- Offenders reported feeling a significant reduction in shame and guilt after the mediation sessions, having had the opportunity to express their remorse and make amends.

- The process fostered empathy and understanding, leading to positive behavioral changes and improved relationships with victims.

Analysis:

- The program successfully helped offenders navigate their emotions by providing a safe space for expression and guided reflection.

- The supportive environment and focus on making amends were crucial for addressing shame and guilt constructively.

Case Study 2: Restorative Circle for Theft

Background:

- A restorative justice program was introduced to address theft cases, with an emphasis on managing the emotional risks for offenders.

Implementation:

- The program included restorative circles where offenders, victims, and community members engaged in dialogue about the impact of the theft.

- Offenders participated in support groups and counseling sessions to help them process their shame and guilt.

Outcomes:

- Offenders demonstrated increased self-awareness and empathy, leading to reduced recidivism rates and positive behavioral changes.

- The process helped restore trust between offenders and the community, fostering a sense of redemption and belonging.

Analysis:

- The restorative circles effectively addressed the emotional risks for offenders by promoting empathy, self-awareness, and community support.

- The combination of dialogue, support groups, and counseling provided a comprehensive approach to managing shame and guilt.

Challenges and Considerations

Balancing Accountability and Support

- Accountability: Ensuring that offenders take responsibility for their actions without becoming overwhelmed by shame and guilt.

- Support: Providing adequate support to help offenders navigate their emotions and use them constructively for personal growth.

Addressing Diverse Needs

- Individualized Approaches: Recognizing that offenders have diverse emotional needs and providing tailored support to address their specific challenges.

- Cultural Sensitivity: Facilitators must be culturally sensitive, acknowledging that cultural factors can influence how shame and guilt are experienced and expressed.

Shame and guilt are significant emotional risks for offenders participating in restorative justice processes. However, with proper support and guidance, these emotions can be navigated constructively, leading to personal growth, behavioral change, and improved relationships. Understanding the nature and impact of shame and guilt, and implementing effective strategies to manage these emotions, is crucial for creating a supportive and effective restorative justice environment. As we continue to explore the risks and challenges of restorative justice in this book, the insights gained from addressing shame and guilt will inform our broader discussion on creating compassionate and effective restorative justice programs.

Stigma: Addressing the Social Stigma That May Persist Even After Reconciliation

Introduction

While restorative justice offers a pathway to healing and reconciliation, offenders often face lingering social stigma even after they have taken responsibility for their actions and made amends. This chapter explores the nature of stigma, its impact on offenders and communities, and strategies for addressing and mitigating its effects within the context of restorative justice.

Understanding Stigma

Definition of Stigma

Stigma refers to the social disapproval or discrimination that individuals face due to characteristics or behaviors that are deemed undesirable or morally wrong by society. In the context of crime, stigma is often associated with:

- Criminal Labels: Being labeled as a "criminal" or "offender," which can lead to negative perceptions and treatment.

- Social Exclusion: The experience of being ostracized or excluded from social, professional, and community activities.

Types of Stigma

Stigma can manifest in various forms, including:

- Public Stigma: Negative attitudes and beliefs held by the general public towards individuals who have committed crimes.

- Self-Stigma: Internalized negative beliefs and feelings of shame and worthlessness experienced by offenders.

- Structural Stigma: Institutional policies and practices that perpetuate discrimination and limit opportunities for offenders.

The Impact of Stigma on Offenders

Emotional and Psychological Effects

The emotional and psychological effects of stigma on offenders can be profound:

- Low Self-Esteem: Stigma can erode an offender's self-esteem, leading to feelings of worthlessness and depression.

- Isolation: The experience of stigma can lead to social isolation, where offenders feel disconnected from their communities and support networks.

Behavioral Consequences

Stigma can influence offenders' behavior in various ways:

- Recidivism: The lack of social acceptance and support can increase the likelihood of reoffending, as offenders may turn to crime as a means of coping or survival.

- Avoidance: Offenders may avoid seeking help or participating in community activities due to fear of judgment and rejection.

Addressing Stigma in Restorative Justice

Community Education and Awareness

Educating the community about restorative justice and the importance of reintegration is crucial for addressing stigma:

- Public Awareness Campaigns: Implementing campaigns that highlight the benefits of restorative justice and the value of supporting offenders' reintegration.

- Community Workshops: Conducting workshops and training sessions for community members to foster empathy and understanding towards offenders.

Supportive Practices

Implementing supportive practices within restorative justice processes can help mitigate stigma:

- Community Involvement: Encouraging community members to actively participate in restorative justice processes, fostering a sense of shared responsibility and support.

- Recognition of Positive Change: Publicly recognizing and celebrating the positive changes and achievements of offenders, reinforcing their value and potential.

Role of Facilitators

Creating a Safe Environment

Facilitators play a key role in creating a safe and supportive environment for offenders:

- Non-Judgmental Approach: Adopting a non-judgmental and empathetic approach, ensuring that offenders feel respected and valued throughout the process.

- Confidentiality: Maintaining confidentiality to protect offenders from undue public scrutiny and judgment.

Ongoing Support and Advocacy

Providing ongoing support and advocacy for offenders is essential for addressing stigma:

- Counseling and Therapy: Offering access to counseling and therapy to help offenders cope with the emotional and psychological effects of stigma.

- Support Groups: Facilitating support groups where offenders can share their experiences and receive encouragement from others who understand their challenges.

Case Studies

Case Study 1: Community Restorative Circle for Theft

Background:

- A restorative justice program was implemented to address theft cases in a rural community.

Implementation:

- The program included community restorative circles where offenders, victims, and community members engaged in dialogue about the impact of the theft and the needs of all participants.

- Public awareness campaigns were conducted to educate the community about restorative justice and the importance of reintegration.

Outcomes:

- Offenders reported feeling more accepted and supported by the community, with reduced experiences of stigma.

- The program led to strengthened community relationships and reduced recidivism rates.

Analysis:

- The combination of restorative circles and community education effectively addressed stigma by fostering empathy and understanding.

- Public recognition of positive changes in offenders helped to reinforce their value and potential within the community.

Case Study 2: Victim-Offender Mediation for Assault

Background:

- A restorative justice program was introduced to address assault cases in an urban neighborhood, with a focus on mitigating stigma.

Implementation:

- Facilitators created a safe and supportive environment for mediation, ensuring confidentiality and respect for all participants.

- Ongoing support and advocacy were provided, including access to counseling and participation in support groups.

Outcomes:

- Offenders demonstrated increased self-esteem and confidence, with a sense of acceptance and belonging within the community.

- The process helped to rebuild trust and reduce stigma, leading to positive behavioral changes and improved relationships.

Analysis:

- The supportive environment and focus on ongoing support were crucial for addressing stigma and promoting positive outcomes for offenders.

- The involvement of facilitators in creating a non-judgmental space and providing advocacy was key to reducing the emotional and psychological impact of stigma.

Challenges and Considerations

Balancing Accountability and Compassion

- Accountability: Ensuring that offenders take responsibility for their actions while also addressing the harmful effects of stigma.

- Compassion: Fostering a compassionate approach that supports offenders' reintegration and personal growth.

Addressing Structural Stigma

- Policy Changes: Advocating for changes in institutional policies and practices that perpetuate stigma and discrimination against offenders.

- Access to Opportunities: Ensuring that offenders have access to education, employment, and housing opportunities to support their reintegration and reduce stigma.

Addressing the social stigma that offenders face, even after reconciliation, is a critical aspect of restorative justice. By educating the community, implementing supportive practices, and providing ongoing support and advocacy, restorative justice can help mitigate the harmful effects of stigma and promote successful reintegration. Understanding the nature and impact of stigma, and implementing effective strategies to address it, is crucial for creating a supportive and effective restorative justice environment. As we continue to explore the risks and challenges of restorative justice in this book, the insights gained from addressing stigma will inform our broader discussion on creating compassionate and effective restorative justice programs.

Addressing Power Imbalances

Facilitator Training: The Importance of Skilled Facilitators in Managing Power Imbalances

Introduction

Restorative justice processes must carefully navigate power dynamics to ensure fair and equitable participation for all parties involved. Facilitators play a crucial role in managing these dynamics, making their training and skill development paramount. This chapter explores the importance of facilitator training in addressing power imbalances, the essential skills required, and strategies for effective facilitator training programs.

The Role of Facilitators in Restorative Justice

Mediating Conflicts

Facilitators are responsible for mediating conflicts and guiding restorative justice processes:

- Neutral Third Party: Facilitators act as neutral third parties, ensuring that discussions remain balanced and respectful.

- Structured Dialogue: They guide structured dialogues, allowing all participants to share their perspectives and feelings.

Ensuring Equitable Participation

Facilitators must ensure that all participants have an equal opportunity to contribute:

- Managing Dominance: Preventing dominant individuals from overpowering the conversation.

- Encouraging Participation: Encouraging quieter or less confident participants to share their views.

Importance of Managing Power Imbalances

Ensuring Fairness

Managing power imbalances is crucial for ensuring fairness in restorative justice processes:

- Equitable Voices: All participants, including victims, offenders, and community members, should have their voices heard equally.

- Balanced Outcomes: Fair outcomes are more likely to be achieved when power dynamics are effectively managed.

Building Trust

Effective management of power dynamics builds trust among participants:

- Trust in Process: Participants are more likely to trust the restorative justice process when they feel their input is valued and respected.

- Trust in Facilitators: Skilled facilitators who manage power imbalances effectively gain the trust of participants, which is essential for successful outcomes.

Essential Skills for Facilitators

Active Listening

Active listening is a fundamental skill for facilitators:

- Understanding Perspectives: Facilitators must listen carefully to understand the perspectives and emotions of all participants.

- Validation: By validating participants' feelings and experiences, facilitators can help balance power dynamics and foster a supportive environment.

Conflict Resolution

Conflict resolution skills are crucial for managing disagreements and maintaining a constructive dialogue:

- De-escalation Techniques: Facilitators must be adept at de-escalating tense situations to prevent conflicts from escalating.

- Mediation Skills: They should be able to mediate disputes and guide participants towards mutually agreeable solutions.

Cultural Competence

Cultural competence is essential for addressing power imbalances related to cultural and social differences:

- Awareness: Facilitators must be aware of cultural and social dynamics that may influence power relations.

- Sensitivity: They should approach cultural differences with sensitivity and respect, ensuring that all participants feel understood and valued.

Strategies for Effective Facilitator Training

Comprehensive Training Programs

Comprehensive training programs are essential for developing the necessary skills in facilitators:

- Curriculum Development: Training programs should include modules on active listening, conflict resolution, cultural competence, and other essential skills.

- Practical Exercises: Facilitators should engage in practical exercises, such as role-playing and simulations, to apply their skills in realistic scenarios.

Ongoing Professional Development

Ongoing professional development ensures that facilitators continue to refine and expand their skills:

- Workshops and Seminars: Regular workshops and seminars on advanced topics and emerging practices in restorative justice.

- Peer Learning: Facilitators can learn from each other through peer learning opportunities, such as discussion groups and collaborative projects.

Supervision and Mentorship

Supervision and mentorship provide additional support and guidance for facilitators:

- Experienced Mentors: Pairing new facilitators with experienced mentors who can offer advice and feedback.

- Regular Supervision: Regular supervision sessions to discuss challenges, reflect on experiences, and receive constructive feedback.

Case Studies

Case Study 1: Restorative Circle for Domestic Violence

Background:

- A restorative justice program was implemented to address domestic violence cases, with a focus on managing power imbalances.

Implementation:

- Facilitators underwent comprehensive training programs, including modules on active listening, conflict resolution, and cultural competence.

- Experienced mentors provided ongoing supervision and support for facilitators throughout the process.

Outcomes:

- Facilitators effectively managed power dynamics, ensuring that all participants had an equal opportunity to share their perspectives.

- The program resulted in fair and balanced outcomes, with participants reporting high levels of trust in the facilitators and the process.

Analysis:

- The comprehensive training and mentorship provided facilitators with the skills and support needed to manage power imbalances effectively.

- The emphasis on cultural competence and conflict resolution was particularly important for addressing the complexities of domestic violence cases.

Case Study 2: Victim-Offender Mediation for Theft

Background:

- A restorative justice program was introduced to address theft cases in an urban community, focusing on equitable participation.

Implementation:

- Facilitators participated in intensive training programs, including practical exercises and role-playing to develop their skills.

- Ongoing professional development opportunities, such as workshops and peer learning sessions, were provided.

Outcomes:

- Facilitators successfully navigated power dynamics, ensuring that victims, offenders, and community members could contribute equally.

- The program led to positive outcomes, with participants feeling heard, respected, and satisfied with the process.

Analysis:

- The intensive training and ongoing professional development were crucial for equipping facilitators with the skills needed to manage power imbalances.

- Practical exercises and peer learning opportunities helped facilitators apply their skills in real-world scenarios.

Challenges and Considerations

Balancing Authority and Neutrality

- Maintaining Neutrality: Facilitators must maintain neutrality while managing power dynamics, avoiding taking sides or showing bias.

- Exerting Authority: They must also exert authority when necessary to ensure that the process remains fair and balanced.

Adapting to Diverse Contexts

- Context-Specific Training: Training programs should be adaptable to diverse contexts, recognizing that power dynamics can vary widely across different communities and cases.

- Continuous Adaptation: Facilitators must be flexible and adaptable, continuously refining their approach based on the specific needs and dynamics of each case.

Conclusion

Managing power imbalances is a critical aspect of restorative justice, and skilled facilitators are essential for ensuring fair and equitable participation. Comprehensive training, ongoing professional development, and support through supervision and mentorship are crucial for equipping facilitators with the skills needed to navigate power dynamics effectively. Understanding the importance of facilitator training and implementing effective strategies is vital for creating a supportive and effective restorative justice environment. As we continue to explore the risks and challenges of restorative justice in this book, the insights gained from addressing power imbalances will inform our broader discussion on creating equitable and compassionate restorative justice programs.

Inclusivity: Ensuring All Voices Are Heard and Respected

Inclusivity is a fundamental principle of restorative justice, ensuring that all participants—victims, offenders, and community members—have their voices heard and respected. This principle is crucial for achieving fair and meaningful outcomes. This chapter explores the importance of inclusivity in restorative justice, strategies for fostering an inclusive environment, and the challenges and considerations involved in ensuring all voices are heard and respected.

The Importance of Inclusivity in Restorative Justice

Equitable Participation

Inclusivity ensures that all participants can equally contribute to the restorative justice process:

- Empowerment: Providing a platform for all voices empowers participants, fostering a sense of ownership and engagement.

- Fair Outcomes: Inclusive processes are more likely to result in fair and balanced outcomes, as diverse perspectives are considered.

Building Trust and Respect

Inclusivity helps build trust and respect among participants:

- Mutual Understanding: Encouraging diverse voices fosters mutual understanding and empathy, essential for healing and reconciliation.

- Respect: Ensuring that all voices are heard and respected reinforces the dignity of each participant and builds trust in the process.

Strategies for Fostering Inclusivity

Skilled Facilitation

Facilitators play a crucial role in fostering an inclusive environment:

- Active Listening: Facilitators should practice active listening, ensuring that all participants feel heard and understood.

- Encouraging Participation: Facilitators must encourage participation from all individuals, particularly those who may feel marginalized or less confident.

Creating Safe Spaces

Creating safe and supportive spaces is essential for inclusivity:

- Non-Judgmental Environment: Establishing a non-judgmental environment where participants can express themselves freely without fear of criticism or retribution.

- Confidentiality: Maintaining confidentiality to protect participants' privacy and encourage open dialogue.

Addressing Power Imbalances

Effective management of power imbalances is critical for ensuring inclusivity:

- Balancing Dynamics: Facilitators should be aware of and address any power imbalances that may inhibit equitable participation.

- Supporting Marginalized Voices: Providing additional support and encouragement to marginalized participants to ensure their voices are heard.

Practical Approaches to Inclusivity

Restorative Circles

Restorative circles are designed to foster inclusivity by promoting equal participation:

- Talking Piece: Using a talking piece can help ensure that everyone has an opportunity to speak without interruption.

- Round-Robin Format: Implementing a round-robin format where each participant takes turns speaking can help ensure that all voices are heard.

Victim-Offender Mediation

Victim-offender mediation can be structured to promote inclusivity:

- Pre-Mediation Meetings: Holding pre-mediation meetings with each participant to understand their perspectives and concerns, ensuring they feel prepared and supported.

- Guided Dialogue: Facilitators guiding the dialogue to ensure balanced participation and prevent domination by any one party.

Benefits of Inclusivity

Enhanced Outcomes

Inclusivity leads to enhanced outcomes for all participants:

- Comprehensive Understanding: Considering diverse perspectives provides a more comprehensive understanding of the issues and impacts, leading to more effective solutions.

- Satisfaction and Buy-In: Participants are more likely to be satisfied with and committed to the outcomes when they feel their voices have been heard and respected.

Strengthened Relationships

Inclusivity helps strengthen relationships within the community:

- Building Bridges: Encouraging open and respectful dialogue fosters mutual understanding and respect, building bridges between individuals and groups.

- Community Cohesion: Inclusive processes promote community cohesion and resilience by reinforcing the value and dignity of each member.

Case Studies

Case Study 1: Restorative Circle for Community Conflict

Background:

- A restorative justice program was implemented to address community conflicts in a diverse urban neighborhood.

Implementation:

- The program used restorative circles with a talking piece and round-robin format to ensure equal participation.

- Facilitators received training in active listening and managing power dynamics.

Outcomes:

- Participants reported feeling heard and respected, with high levels of satisfaction and commitment to the outcomes.

- The process led to a deeper understanding of the issues and strengthened relationships within the community.

Analysis:

- The use of restorative circles and skilled facilitation effectively promoted inclusivity, ensuring that all voices were heard and respected.

- The inclusive approach contributed to fair and meaningful outcomes, enhancing community cohesion.

Case Study 2: Victim-Offender Mediation for Juvenile Offenses

Background:

- A restorative justice program was introduced to address juvenile offenses, focusing on inclusivity and equitable participation.

Implementation:

- Facilitators held pre-mediation meetings with each participant to understand their perspectives and prepare them for the mediation.

- The mediation sessions were structured to encourage balanced participation, with facilitators guiding the dialogue.

Outcomes:

- Participants, including juveniles and their families, felt empowered and respected, leading to positive behavioral changes and reconciliation.

- The process fostered empathy and understanding, reducing recidivism and strengthening family relationships.

Analysis:

- The structured approach to victim-offender mediation and pre-mediation meetings ensured that all voices were heard and respected.

- The inclusive process led to meaningful outcomes, promoting healing and reducing future offenses.

Challenges and Considerations

Overcoming Barriers to Participation

Facilitators must be aware of and address barriers to participation:

- Language and Communication: Providing language support and ensuring clear communication to include participants with different linguistic backgrounds.

- Accessibility: Ensuring that restorative justice processes are accessible to participants with disabilities or other barriers.

Ensuring Cultural Sensitivity

Cultural sensitivity is essential for fostering inclusivity:

- Cultural Awareness: Facilitators should be aware of and respect cultural differences that may influence participation and communication styles.

- Tailored Approaches: Adapting restorative justice practices to align with the cultural norms and values of the participants.

Inclusivity is a cornerstone of restorative justice, ensuring that all voices are heard and respected. By implementing strategies such as skilled facilitation, creating safe spaces, and addressing power imbalances, restorative justice processes can foster equitable participation and meaningful outcomes. Understanding the importance of inclusivity and adopting effective approaches is crucial for creating a supportive and effective restorative justice environment. As we continue to explore the risks and challenges of restorative justice in this book, the insights gained from promoting inclusivity will inform our broader discussion on creating fair and compassionate restorative justice programs.

CHAPTER 07

IMPLEMENTING RESTORATIVE JUSTICE

Best Practices

Effective implementation of restorative justice is critical for achieving meaningful outcomes and ensuring the well-being of all participants. Adhering to best practices, such as adequate preparation of participants and ensuring ongoing support and follow-up, is essential for the success of restorative justice programs. This chapter explores these best practices in detail, providing guidelines for practitioners to enhance the efficacy and impact of restorative justice processes.

Preparation: Adequate Preparation of All Participants

Importance of Preparation

Adequate preparation is a foundational element of successful restorative justice:

- Building Trust: Preparation helps build trust between facilitators and participants, creating a safe environment for open dialogue.

- Setting Expectations: Clear communication about the process and expectations helps participants feel more comfortable and engaged.

Steps for Effective Preparation

Initial Assessment

Conducting an initial assessment is crucial for understanding the needs and readiness of participants:

- Emotional Readiness: Assessing the emotional readiness of both victims and offenders to ensure they are prepared to engage in the restorative process.

- Understanding Expectations: Discussing expectations with participants to align their understanding and set realistic goals for the process.

Providing Information

Providing comprehensive information about the restorative justice process is essential:

- Process Overview: Explaining the steps involved in the restorative justice process, including the roles of facilitators, victims, offenders, and community members.

- Potential Outcomes: Discussing potential outcomes and emphasizing the importance of flexibility and openness to different resolutions.

Emotional and Practical Support

Offering emotional and practical support during the preparation phase helps participants feel supported and empowered:

- Counseling Services: Providing access to counseling services to help participants process their emotions and prepare for the restorative process.

- Logistical Support: Assisting with practical needs, such as transportation and scheduling, to ensure that participants can attend sessions without undue stress.

Case Study: Preparation for Victim-Offender Mediation

Background:

- A restorative justice program aimed at addressing property crimes through victim-offender mediation.

Implementation:

- Facilitators conducted initial assessments to gauge the emotional readiness of victims and offenders.

- Comprehensive information sessions were held to explain the mediation process and set realistic expectations.

- Emotional and practical support, including counseling and logistical assistance, was provided to all participants.

Outcomes:

- Participants reported feeling well-prepared and supported, leading to more meaningful and effective mediation sessions.

- The program achieved high levels of satisfaction and positive outcomes, including reduced recidivism and improved relationships.

Analysis:

- The thorough preparation phase was crucial for the success of the mediation process, ensuring that all participants were ready and informed.

Follow-up: Ensuring Ongoing Support and Follow-up After the Initial Process

Importance of Follow-up

Ongoing support and follow-up are essential for sustaining the benefits of restorative justice:

- Maintaining Progress: Ensuring that the progress made during the initial process is maintained and built upon.

- Addressing Challenges: Providing support to address any challenges or issues that arise after the initial process.

Steps for Effective Follow-up

Scheduled Check-ins

Regular check-ins with participants help monitor their progress and provide ongoing support:

- Periodic Meetings: Scheduling periodic follow-up meetings with participants to discuss their progress, address any concerns, and provide additional support as needed.

- Feedback Mechanisms: Implementing feedback mechanisms to gather input from participants about their experiences and any ongoing needs.

Continued Support Services

Providing continued access to support services is crucial for long-term success:

- Counseling and Therapy: Offering ongoing counseling and therapy services to help participants cope with any residual emotional or psychological issues.

- Community Resources: Connecting participants with community resources, such as support groups and educational programs, to foster continued growth and reintegration.

Monitoring and Evaluation

Monitoring and evaluating the outcomes of the restorative justice process help ensure its effectiveness and identify areas for improvement:

- Outcome Tracking: Tracking key outcomes, such as recidivism rates, participant satisfaction, and relationship improvements, to assess the impact of the process.

- Program Evaluation: Conducting regular program evaluations to identify strengths and areas for improvement, ensuring that the restorative justice program remains effective and responsive to participants' needs.

Case Study: Follow-up for Restorative Circles

Background:

- A restorative justice program using restorative circles to address community conflicts in a diverse urban neighborhood.

Implementation:

- Scheduled regular check-ins with participants to monitor their progress and provide ongoing support.

- Continued access to counseling services and community resources was provided to all participants.

- Outcomes were tracked, and regular program evaluations were conducted to ensure the effectiveness of the restorative circles.

Outcomes:

- Participants reported sustained improvements in relationships and a continued sense of support and community cohesion.

- The program achieved long-term success, with reduced recidivism and enhanced community resilience.

Analysis:

- The comprehensive follow-up phase was essential for maintaining the benefits of the restorative circles and supporting participants' ongoing needs.

Best Practices for Implementing Restorative Justice

Comprehensive Training for Facilitators

Ensuring that facilitators are well-trained is crucial for the success of restorative justice programs:

- Skills Development: Providing training in active listening, conflict resolution, and cultural competence to equip facilitators with the necessary skills.

- Ongoing Professional Development: Offering regular professional development opportunities to help facilitators refine their skills and stay updated on best practices.

Community Involvement

Involving the community in restorative justice processes enhances their effectiveness and sustainability:

- Engagement Strategies: Implementing strategies to engage community members, such as public awareness campaigns and community workshops.

- Collaborative Approaches: Encouraging collaborative approaches that involve community members in the planning and implementation of restorative justice programs.

Cultural Sensitivity

Ensuring cultural sensitivity is essential for fostering inclusivity and respect:

- Cultural Awareness Training: Providing cultural awareness training for facilitators and participants to promote understanding and respect for diverse backgrounds.

- Tailored Practices: Adapting restorative justice practices to align with the cultural norms and values of participants.

Conclusion

Effective implementation of restorative justice requires adherence to best practices, including thorough preparation of participants and ensuring ongoing support and follow-up. These practices are essential for achieving meaningful outcomes and fostering the well-being of all participants. By focusing on comprehensive preparation, regular follow-up, and continuous support, restorative justice programs can create a supportive and effective environment for healing and reconciliation. Understanding and implementing these best practices is crucial for creating fair, inclusive, and compassionate restorative justice programs. As we continue to explore the implementation of restorative justice in this book, the insights gained from these best practices will inform our broader discussion on creating successful and impactful restorative justice initiatives.

Case Studies

Introduction

Real-world examples provide valuable insights into the practical application and outcomes of restorative justice. This chapter presents case studies that highlight both the successes and lessons learned from various restorative justice initiatives. These case studies offer a comprehensive understanding of how restorative justice can be effectively implemented and the impact it can have on individuals and communities.

Success Stories

Case Study 1: Youth Offender Program

Background:

- A youth offender program was implemented in a suburban community to address minor offenses such as vandalism and theft. The program focused on victim-offender mediation and community service.

Implementation:

- Offenders participated in mediation sessions with their victims, facilitated by trained mediators. The sessions aimed to foster understanding and empathy, allowing offenders to acknowledge the harm they caused and work towards making amends.

- As part of their reparation plan, offenders engaged in community service projects, which provided an opportunity to contribute positively to their community and rebuild trust.

Outcomes:

- Reduced Recidivism: The program reported a significant reduction in recidivism rates among participating youth offenders, with many showing long-term behavioral improvements.

- Enhanced Empathy: Offenders developed a deeper understanding of the impact of their actions, leading to increased empathy and remorse.

- Community Healing: The program fostered stronger relationships within the community, with victims and offenders working together towards common goals.

Analysis:

- The success of this program can be attributed to the focus on victim-offender mediation and the integration of community service. These elements provided a holistic approach to addressing harm and promoting healing.

Case Study 2: Domestic Violence Restorative Circle

Background:

- A restorative justice program was introduced in an urban setting to address domestic violence cases. The program utilized restorative circles to facilitate dialogue and healing among victims, offenders, and community members.

Implementation:

- Participants attended pre-circle preparation sessions to ensure they were emotionally ready and informed about the process. Trained facilitators guided the restorative circles, promoting a safe and respectful environment for open dialogue.

- The circles allowed victims to share their experiences and feelings, while offenders had the opportunity to express remorse and commit to behavioral change. Community members provided additional support and perspectives.

Outcomes:

- Emotional Healing: Victims reported significant emotional healing and a sense of empowerment from being heard and validated.

- Behavioral Change: Offenders demonstrated genuine remorse and a commitment to change, with many participating in ongoing counseling and support programs.

- Strengthened Community: The program helped rebuild trust and fostered a supportive community network, contributing to long-term resilience and cohesion.

Analysis:

- The program's success was due to the comprehensive preparation of participants and the emphasis on creating a safe, inclusive space for dialogue. The involvement of community members also played a crucial role in supporting both victims and offenders.

Case Study 3: School-Based Restorative Justice Program

Background:

- A restorative justice program was implemented in a high school to address bullying and conflicts among students. The program aimed to create a positive school environment and reduce disciplinary issues.

Implementation:

- The program used restorative circles and peer mediation to address incidents of bullying and conflict. Trained student mediators and facilitators worked with their peers to resolve issues and develop reparation plans.

- Regular workshops and training sessions were conducted to educate students and staff about restorative practices and promote a culture of respect and empathy.

Outcomes:

- Improved School Climate: The program led to a noticeable improvement in the school climate, with a decrease in bullying incidents and disciplinary referrals.

- Student Empowerment: Students felt empowered to take responsibility for their actions and contribute to a positive school environment.

- Enhanced Relationships: The program fostered stronger relationships among students, staff, and the wider school community, promoting mutual respect and understanding.

Analysis:

- The success of the school-based program was largely due to the involvement of students in the mediation process and the focus on education and awareness. Empowering students to take an active role in resolving conflicts created a sense of ownership and accountability.

Lessons Learned

Lesson 1: Importance of Comprehensive Preparation

Key Takeaways:

- Comprehensive preparation of participants is crucial for the success of restorative justice processes. Ensuring that victims, offenders, and community members are emotionally ready and well-informed helps create a supportive environment for dialogue and healing.

- Pre-session counseling, informational meetings, and logistical support are essential components of effective preparation.

Case Study Example:

- The Domestic Violence Restorative Circle program's success was significantly enhanced by the thorough preparation of participants, which helped build trust and readiness for the process.

Lesson 2: Role of Skilled Facilitators

Key Takeaways:

- Skilled facilitators are essential for managing power dynamics, fostering inclusivity, and guiding the restorative process effectively. Facilitators must be trained in active listening, conflict resolution, and cultural competence.

- Ongoing professional development and support for facilitators ensure they remain effective in their roles.

Case Study Example:

- In the Youth Offender Program, the role of skilled mediators was pivotal in facilitating productive dialogues and ensuring that all participants felt heard and respected.

Lesson 3: Community Involvement and Support

Key Takeaways:

- Involving the community in restorative justice processes enhances their effectiveness and sustainability. Community members provide additional perspectives and support, fostering a sense of shared responsibility and healing.

- Public awareness campaigns and community workshops help build understanding and support for restorative justice initiatives.

Case Study Example:

- The success of the School-Based Restorative Justice Program was bolstered by the active involvement of students, staff, and the wider school community, promoting a culture of empathy and respect.

Lesson 4: Ongoing Support and Follow-up

Key Takeaways:

- Ensuring ongoing support and follow-up after the initial restorative process is crucial for maintaining progress and addressing any emerging challenges. Regular check-ins, access to counseling, and community resources are vital components of continued support.

- Monitoring and evaluating outcomes help identify areas for improvement and ensure the long-term success of restorative justice programs.

Case Study Example:

- The follow-up phase of the Domestic Violence Restorative Circle program, including regular check-ins and continued access to support services, was essential for sustaining the positive outcomes achieved during the initial process.

Conclusion

Real-world case studies illustrate the practical application and outcomes of restorative justice, highlighting both successes and lessons learned. These examples underscore the importance of comprehensive preparation, skilled facilitation, community involvement, and ongoing support in achieving meaningful and sustainable outcomes. By understanding and implementing these best practices, restorative justice programs can effectively promote healing, reconciliation, and positive change for individuals and communities. As we continue to explore the implementation of restorative justice in this book, the insights gained from these case studies will inform our broader discussion on creating successful and impactful restorative justice initiatives.

Training Facilitators

Skilled facilitators are essential for the success of restorative justice circles, as they guide the process, manage dynamics, and ensure that all voices are heard and respected.

This chapter explores effective training methods for facilitators and the importance of continuous development and support to maintain high standards and adapt to evolving needs.

Training Programs: Effective Training Methods for Facilitators

Core Components of Facilitator Training

Effective facilitator training programs must cover several core components to equip facilitators with the necessary skills and knowledge:

Active Listening and Communication

- Active Listening: Facilitators must be trained to listen attentively, validate participants' feelings, and respond empathetically.

- Effective Communication: Training should focus on clear, respectful, and non-judgmental communication techniques.

Conflict Resolution and Mediation

- Conflict Resolution: Facilitators need skills to manage and de-escalate conflicts, ensuring a safe and constructive dialogue.

- Mediation Techniques: Training should include mediation strategies that help parties reach mutual understanding and agreements.

Cultural Competence and Sensitivity

- Cultural Awareness: Facilitators should be aware of cultural differences and sensitive to the diverse backgrounds of participants.

- Inclusivity Practices: Training should emphasize practices that promote inclusivity and respect for all cultural perspectives.

Training Methods and Approaches

Interactive Workshops

- Role-Playing Exercises: Simulated scenarios allow facilitators to practice and refine their skills in a controlled environment.

- Group Discussions: Facilitators can share experiences and learn from each other through guided discussions and feedback sessions.

Mentorship and Supervision

- Experienced Mentors: Pairing new facilitators with experienced mentors provides guidance, support, and practical insights.

- Regular Supervision: Ongoing supervision helps facilitators reflect on their practice, address challenges, and receive constructive feedback.

Case Studies and Real-Life Examples

- Analyzing Case Studies: Reviewing and analyzing real-life case studies helps facilitators understand the complexities and nuances of restorative justice processes.

- Learning from Experience: Facilitators can learn valuable lessons from the successes and challenges of past cases.

Comprehensive Training Programs

Example Program: Basic Facilitator Training Course

Overview:

- A six-week course designed to provide foundational skills for new facilitators.

Modules:

1. Introduction to Restorative Justice: Understanding the principles and goals of restorative justice.

2. Active Listening and Communication: Developing skills for effective listening and communication.

3. Conflict Resolution: Techniques for managing and resolving conflicts.

4. Cultural Competence: Strategies for promoting inclusivity and cultural sensitivity.

5. Practical Application: Role-playing exercises and simulated scenarios.

6. Supervision and Mentorship: Ongoing support through mentorship and supervision.

Outcomes:

- Facilitators complete the course with a solid foundation of skills and knowledge, ready to begin facilitating restorative justice circles.

Continuous Development: Ongoing Education and Support for Facilitators

Importance of Continuous Development

Continuous development is essential for facilitators to maintain and enhance their skills:

- Adapting to Changes: Restorative justice practices evolve, and facilitators need to stay updated on new methodologies and approaches.

- Addressing Challenges: Ongoing education helps facilitators address emerging challenges and improve their practice.

Strategies for Continuous Development

Advanced Training and Specialization

- Advanced Workshops: Offering advanced workshops on specific topics, such as trauma-informed care or advanced mediation techniques.

- Specialization Tracks: Facilitators can specialize in areas like domestic violence, youth justice, or community conflicts, gaining deeper expertise.

Regular Reflection and Supervision

- Reflective Practice: Facilitators should engage in regular reflective practice to evaluate their experiences and identify areas for improvement.

- Supervision Sessions: Regular supervision sessions provide a space for facilitators to discuss challenges, receive feedback, and develop their skills further.

Professional Development Opportunities

- Conferences and Seminars: Attending restorative justice conferences and seminars to learn about the latest research, trends, and best practices.

- Peer Learning Groups: Facilitators can participate in peer learning groups to share experiences, challenges, and solutions with colleagues.

Access to Resources and Support

- Resource Libraries: Providing access to resource libraries with books, articles, and online courses on restorative justice.

- Support Networks: Establishing support networks where facilitators can seek advice, share experiences, and find encouragement from peers.

Example Program: Ongoing Professional Development for Facilitators

Overview:

- A continuous professional development program designed to support facilitators in their ongoing growth.

Components:

1. Monthly Workshops: Advanced workshops on specialized topics.

2. Supervision Groups: Regular supervision sessions facilitated by experienced practitioners.

3. Annual Conferences: Participation in national and international restorative justice conferences.

4. Peer Learning Circles: Small groups of facilitators who meet regularly to discuss experiences and share insights.

5. Online Resource Portal: Access to a comprehensive online portal with educational materials and resources.

Outcomes:

- Facilitators remain engaged, informed, and supported, continually enhancing their skills and adapting to new challenges.

Skilled facilitators are crucial to the success of restorative justice circles, and their training and continuous development are essential for maintaining high standards of practice. Effective training programs that cover core competencies, utilize interactive methods, and provide comprehensive support are foundational for preparing facilitators. Continuous development through advanced training, reflective practice, professional opportunities, and support networks ensures that facilitators can adapt to changes and address challenges effectively. By investing in the training and ongoing development of facilitators, restorative justice programs can achieve meaningful and lasting outcomes for all participants. As we continue to explore the implementation of restorative justice in this book, the insights gained from these best practices in facilitator training will inform our broader discussion on creating successful and impactful restorative justice initiatives.

CHAPTER 08

MEASURING THE IMPACT

Qualitative Measures

Participant Feedback: Collecting and Analyzing Feedback from Participants

Measuring the impact of restorative justice is essential for understanding its effectiveness and areas for improvement. One of the most valuable qualitative measures is participant feedback, which provides insights into the experiences, perceptions, and outcomes of those involved in the process. This chapter explores the importance of participant feedback, methods for collecting and analyzing feedback, and how to use this information to enhance restorative justice programs.

Importance of Participant Feedback

Enhancing Program Effectiveness

Participant feedback is crucial for enhancing the effectiveness of restorative justice programs:

- Identifying Strengths and Weaknesses: Feedback helps identify what aspects of the program are working well and what areas need improvement.

- Adapting to Needs: Understanding participants' experiences allows facilitators to adapt and tailor the program to better meet their needs.

Promoting Accountability

Feedback from participants promotes accountability within restorative justice programs:

- Transparency: Collecting and sharing feedback demonstrates a commitment to transparency and continuous improvement.

- Responsiveness: Acting on feedback shows that the program values participants' input and is responsive to their concerns and suggestions.

Building Trust and Engagement

Participant feedback helps build trust and engagement:

- Empowerment: Soliciting feedback empowers participants, making them feel valued and heard.

- Enhanced Participation: When participants see that their feedback leads to positive changes, they are more likely to engage meaningfully in the process.

Methods for Collecting Participant Feedback

Surveys and Questionnaires

Surveys and questionnaires are effective tools for collecting structured feedback:

- Pre- and Post-Process Surveys: Administering surveys before and after the restorative justice process can capture changes in participants' perceptions and experiences.

- Standardized Questions: Using standardized questions ensures consistency and allows for comparative analysis over time.

Example Questions:

- How would you rate your overall experience with the restorative justice process?

- Did you feel heard and respected during the sessions?

- How has your perception of the offender/victim changed as a result of this process?

- What aspects of the process were most beneficial for you?

- What improvements would you suggest for the program?

Interviews and Focus Groups

Interviews and focus groups provide deeper, qualitative insights into participants' experiences:

- Individual Interviews: One-on-one interviews allow for in-depth exploration of individual experiences and perspectives.

- Focus Groups: Group discussions can reveal shared experiences and generate ideas for program improvements.

Conducting Effective Interviews and Focus Groups:

- Trained Facilitators: Use trained facilitators to conduct interviews and focus groups, ensuring that discussions are guided effectively and sensitively.

- Open-Ended Questions: Ask open-ended questions to encourage detailed and reflective responses.

- Confidentiality: Ensure confidentiality to create a safe space for honest feedback.

Feedback Forms

Simple feedback forms can be used to gather immediate reactions and suggestions:

- Post-Session Forms: Distribute feedback forms immediately after sessions to capture participants' initial impressions and suggestions.

- Anonymity Options: Allow for anonymous feedback to ensure participants feel comfortable sharing honest opinions.

Example Feedback Form Questions:

- What did you find most valuable about today's session?

- Were there any aspects of the session that you found challenging or unhelpful?

- Do you have any suggestions for improving future sessions?

Analyzing Participant Feedback

Qualitative Analysis Techniques

Analyzing qualitative feedback involves identifying themes, patterns, and insights:

- Thematic Analysis: Categorize feedback into common themes to identify key areas of concern, satisfaction, and suggestions for improvement.

- Coding: Use coding techniques to systematically organize and interpret qualitative data, making it easier to identify recurring themes.

Integrating Feedback into Program Development

Using participant feedback to inform program development is crucial for continuous improvement:

- Action Plans: Develop action plans based on feedback to address identified issues and implement suggested improvements.

- Continuous Monitoring: Regularly review and update action plans to ensure ongoing responsiveness to participant needs and experiences.

Case Studies

Case Study 1: Restorative Circle for Community Conflicts

Background:

- A restorative justice program was implemented to address community conflicts in a diverse urban neighborhood.

Feedback Collection:

- Surveys were administered before and after the process to assess changes in participants' perceptions and experiences.

- Individual interviews were conducted with participants to gather in-depth feedback.

Analysis and Outcomes:

- Thematic analysis of survey and interview data revealed key strengths, such as increased empathy and understanding, and areas for improvement, such as the need for more cultural sensitivity training for facilitators.

- Based on the feedback, the program introduced additional cultural competence training and adjusted the structure of the restorative circles to better accommodate diverse cultural practices.

Impact:

- The changes led to higher participant satisfaction and enhanced the effectiveness of the program in resolving community conflicts.

Case Study 2: Victim-Offender Mediation for Juvenile Offenses

Background:

- A restorative justice program focused on victim-offender mediation for juvenile offenses.

Feedback Collection:

- Feedback forms were distributed after each mediation session to capture immediate reactions and suggestions.

- Focus groups were conducted with both victims and offenders to explore their experiences in more depth.

Analysis and Outcomes:

- Analysis of feedback forms and focus group discussions highlighted the importance of ongoing support for participants and the need for more structured follow-up.

- The program introduced follow-up sessions and additional support resources based on participant feedback.

Impact:

- The enhancements led to improved outcomes, including higher rates of satisfaction among participants and reduced recidivism rates among juvenile offenders.

Best Practices for Collecting and Analyzing Participant Feedback

Ensuring Inclusivity and Representation

- Diverse Voices: Ensure that feedback is collected from a diverse range of participants, including victims, offenders, and community members.

- Accessible Methods: Use accessible methods for collecting feedback to ensure that all participants can contribute, regardless of their literacy levels or language proficiency.

Creating a Safe and Supportive Environment

- Confidentiality: Guarantee confidentiality to encourage honest and open feedback.

- Supportive Facilitation: Use trained facilitators to guide feedback sessions, ensuring that participants feel supported and respected.

Regular Review and Adaptation

- Continuous Improvement: Regularly review feedback and implement necessary changes to improve the program.

- Feedback Loops: Establish feedback loops to inform participants about how their feedback has been used to make improvements, reinforcing their sense of involvement and value.

Participant feedback is a vital qualitative measure for understanding the impact of restorative justice programs. By collecting and analyzing feedback through surveys, interviews, focus groups, and feedback forms, practitioners can gain valuable insights into participants' experiences and perceptions. This information is crucial for enhancing program effectiveness, promoting accountability, and building trust and engagement. By implementing best practices for feedback collection and analysis, restorative justice programs can continuously improve and adapt to meet the needs of all participants, ensuring meaningful and lasting outcomes. As we continue to explore the measurement of restorative justice impact in this book, the insights gained from participant feedback will inform our broader discussion on creating effective and responsive restorative justice initiatives.

Measuring the Impact

Qualitative Measures

Narrative Analysis: Examining Personal Stories and Experiences

Introduction

Narrative analysis is a powerful qualitative method for examining the personal stories and experiences of participants in restorative justice processes. By analyzing narratives, practitioners can gain deep insights into the emotional, psychological, and social impacts of restorative justice on individuals and communities. This chapter explores the importance of narrative analysis, methods for collecting and analyzing narratives, and how to use these insights to improve restorative justice programs.

Importance of Narrative Analysis

Understanding Personal Impact

Narrative analysis helps to understand the personal impact of restorative justice on participants:

- Emotional and Psychological Insights: Personal stories reveal the emotional and psychological experiences of victims, offenders, and community members.

- Holistic Understanding: Narratives provide a holistic understanding of how restorative justice affects individuals' lives, beyond what quantitative measures can capture.

Enhancing Empathy and Connection

Analyzing personal stories enhances empathy and connection among participants and practitioners:

- Shared Humanity: Narratives highlight the shared humanity of participants, fostering empathy and understanding.

- Building Trust: Sharing personal stories builds trust and rapport, strengthening the restorative justice process.

Informing Program Development

Narrative analysis informs program development and improvement:

- Identifying Themes: Analyzing common themes and experiences helps identify strengths and areas for improvement in restorative justice programs.

- Participant-Centered Adjustments: Insights from narratives guide adjustments that better meet the needs and experiences of participants.

Methods for Collecting Narratives

Interviews

Interviews are a primary method for collecting personal stories and experiences:

- In-Depth Interviews: Conducting in-depth, one-on-one interviews allows participants to share their stories in detail.

- Semi-Structured Format: Using a semi-structured format ensures that key topics are covered while allowing participants to express themselves freely.

Example Interview Questions:

- Can you describe your experience with the restorative justice process?

- How did participating in the process affect you emotionally and psychologically?

- What aspects of the process were most meaningful or impactful for you?

- Were there any challenges or difficulties you faced during the process?

Written Narratives

Encouraging participants to write their stories can provide rich narrative data:

- Reflective Essays: Participants can write reflective essays about their experiences with restorative justice.

- Journals: Keeping journals throughout the restorative justice process allows participants to document their thoughts and feelings over time.

Focus Groups

Focus groups can facilitate the sharing of personal stories in a group setting:

- Group Dynamics: The group setting can encourage participants to share their experiences and learn from each other.

- Facilitated Discussions: Skilled facilitators guide the discussion to ensure that all voices are heard and respected.

Story Circles

Story circles are a method of collective storytelling where participants share their experiences in a supportive group:

- Community Building: Story circles foster a sense of community and shared understanding among participants.

- Structured Sharing: Each participant takes turns sharing their story, ensuring that everyone has an opportunity to speak.

Analyzing Narratives

Thematic Analysis

Thematic analysis involves identifying and analyzing common themes within narratives:

- Coding: Assigning codes to specific sections of the narrative to categorize different themes and topics.

- Pattern Recognition: Identifying patterns and recurring themes that emerge across different narratives.

Content Analysis

Content analysis focuses on the frequency and context of specific words, phrases, or concepts within narratives:

- Frequency Counts: Counting the frequency of specific words or phrases to identify key themes and concerns.

- Contextual Analysis: Examining the context in which certain words or concepts are used to understand their meaning and significance.

Structural Analysis

Structural analysis examines the structure and organization of narratives:

- Narrative Structure: Analyzing the overall structure of the narrative, including the beginning, middle, and end.

- Plot and Characters: Examining the plot and characters within the narrative to understand the dynamics and relationships described.

Narrative Synthesis

Narrative synthesis involves integrating insights from multiple narratives to form a comprehensive understanding:

- Cross-Narrative Themes: Identifying themes and patterns that emerge across different narratives to draw broader conclusions.

- Holistic Integration: Combining insights from thematic, content, and structural analyses to create a holistic understanding of participants' experiences.

Case Studies

Case Study 1: Restorative Justice for Juvenile Offenders

Background:

- A restorative justice program focused on juvenile offenders, incorporating narrative analysis to understand the impact on participants.

Narrative Collection:

- In-depth interviews were conducted with juvenile offenders, their families, and victims to gather personal stories and experiences.

- Participants were also encouraged to keep journals documenting their thoughts and feelings throughout the process.

Analysis and Outcomes:

- Thematic analysis revealed common themes of remorse, personal growth, and the importance of family support.

- Content analysis highlighted the frequency of words related to empathy, accountability, and healing.

- Structural analysis provided insights into the narrative arcs of personal transformation and reconciliation.

Impact:

- The findings informed program adjustments, such as incorporating more family involvement and focusing on empathy-building activities.

- Participants reported feeling more understood and supported, leading to better outcomes and reduced recidivism.

Case Study 2: Community Restorative Circles

Background:

- A restorative justice program using community restorative circles to address neighborhood conflicts and foster community cohesion.

Narrative Collection:

- Story circles were held where community members shared their experiences and perspectives on the conflicts and the restorative process.

- Written narratives were also collected from participants who preferred to express their stories in writing.

Analysis and Outcomes:

- Thematic analysis identified themes of community solidarity, mutual respect, and collective healing.

- Content analysis showed frequent references to trust, forgiveness, and future collaboration.

- Structural analysis revealed the progression from initial conflict to resolution and strengthened relationships.

Impact:

- The narrative analysis informed the development of follow-up activities to maintain and build on the positive outcomes.

- The program successfully fostered a sense of community and improved relationships, with participants expressing greater trust and willingness to collaborate.

Best Practices for Narrative Analysis

Ensuring Ethical Considerations

- Informed Consent: Obtain informed consent from participants, ensuring they understand the purpose and use of their narratives.

- Confidentiality: Maintain confidentiality to protect participants' privacy and encourage honest sharing.

Creating a Supportive Environment

- Safe Spaces: Create safe and supportive spaces for participants to share their stories without fear of judgment or retribution.

- Empathetic Facilitation: Use empathetic and skilled facilitators to guide narrative collection and analysis.

Triangulation

- Multiple Methods: Use multiple methods (e.g., interviews, written narratives, story circles) to gather diverse perspectives and enhance the robustness of the analysis.

- Cross-Validation: Validate findings by cross-referencing themes and patterns across different narratives and sources.

Narrative analysis is a powerful tool for understanding the personal stories and experiences of participants in restorative justice processes. By collecting and analyzing narratives through methods such as interviews, written narratives, focus groups, and story circles, practitioners can gain deep insights into the emotional, psychological, and social impacts of restorative justice. These insights are crucial for enhancing program effectiveness, fostering empathy and connection, and informing continuous improvement. By implementing best practices for narrative analysis, restorative justice programs can create meaningful and lasting outcomes for individuals and communities. As we continue to explore the measurement of restorative justice impact in this book, the insights gained from narrative analysis will inform our broader discussion on creating effective and responsive restorative justice initiatives.

Quantitative Measures

Recidivism Rates: Tracking Reoffending Rates Among Participants

Introduction

Quantitative measures are essential for providing a comprehensive understanding of the effectiveness of restorative justice programs. One of the most critical metrics is recidivism rates, which track the reoffending rates among participants. This chapter explores the importance of recidivism as a metric, methods for tracking recidivism, analyzing data, and using insights to improve restorative justice programs.

Importance of Recidivism as a Metric

Indicator of Program Effectiveness

Recidivism rates serve as a key indicator of the effectiveness of restorative justice programs:

- Behavioral Change: Lower recidivism rates suggest that participants have undergone meaningful behavioral change and are less likely to reoffend.

- Long-Term Impact: Tracking recidivism provides insights into the long-term impact of restorative justice interventions on participants.

Justifying Funding and Support

Demonstrating reduced recidivism rates can help justify funding and support for restorative justice programs:

- Evidence-Based Success: Quantitative data showing reduced reoffending rates can be compelling evidence of the program's success to stakeholders and funders.

- Policy Influence: Positive recidivism outcomes can influence policy decisions and promote the broader adoption of restorative justice practices.

Methods for Tracking Recidivism

Data Collection

Accurate data collection is crucial for tracking recidivism rates effectively:

- Official Records: Utilize official criminal justice records, such as police reports, court records, and probation records, to track reoffending.

- Self-Reports: Supplement official records with self-reported data from participants, acknowledging potential limitations and biases.

Example Data Points:

- Number of arrests or charges post-intervention.

- Types of offenses committed post-intervention.

- Time elapsed between intervention and reoffending.

Longitudinal Studies

Longitudinal studies are effective for tracking recidivism over an extended period:

- Baseline Measurement: Establish a baseline by recording participants' criminal history prior to the restorative justice intervention.

- Follow-Up Assessments: Conduct follow-up assessments at regular intervals (e.g., six months, one year, two years) to track reoffending rates.

Example Study Design:

- Cohort of participants who completed the restorative justice program.

- Control group of individuals who did not participate in the program for comparative analysis.

- Periodic follow-up to monitor recidivism and other relevant outcomes.

Comparative Analysis

Comparative analysis with control groups or other justice interventions can provide valuable context:

- Matched Control Groups: Compare recidivism rates of restorative justice participants with a matched control group that did not receive the intervention.

- Alternative Interventions: Compare outcomes with those from alternative interventions, such as traditional criminal justice processes or diversion programs.

Analyzing Recidivism Data

Statistical Analysis

Statistical analysis helps interpret recidivism data and identify significant trends and patterns:

- Descriptive Statistics: Calculate descriptive statistics, such as mean, median, and standard deviation, to summarize recidivism rates.

- Inferential Statistics: Use inferential statistics to determine the significance of differences between groups (e.g., participants vs. control group).

Example Statistical Techniques:

- T-tests or ANOVA to compare mean recidivism rates between groups.

- Regression analysis to identify factors influencing recidivism rates.

Identifying Trends and Patterns

Analyzing recidivism data can reveal trends and patterns that inform program improvements:

- Demographic Analysis: Examine recidivism rates by demographic factors, such as age, gender, and socioeconomic status, to identify at-risk groups.

- Program Features: Analyze which features of the restorative justice program (e.g., type of intervention, duration, facilitator training) are associated with lower recidivism rates.

Reporting Findings

Clear and comprehensive reporting of recidivism findings is essential for transparency and accountability:

- Visualizations: Use visualizations, such as graphs and charts, to present recidivism data clearly and effectively.

- Summary Reports: Prepare summary reports highlighting key findings, trends, and recommendations for stakeholders and funders.

Case Studies

Case Study 1: Youth Restorative Justice Program

Background:

- A restorative justice program aimed at reducing recidivism among youth offenders involved in minor crimes.

Methodology:

- Data Collection: Utilized official records and self-reports to track reoffending rates.

- Longitudinal Study: Conducted follow-up assessments at six months, one year, and two years post-intervention.

- Comparative Analysis: Compared recidivism rates with a control group of youth offenders who went through the traditional justice system.

Findings:

- Significant Reduction: The program reported a 30% reduction in recidivism rates among participants compared to the control group.

- Behavioral Change: Participants showed significant behavioral improvements and reduced involvement in criminal activities.

- Program Features: The most effective program features included family involvement and ongoing support post-intervention.

Impact:

- The positive outcomes justified continued funding and expansion of the program, highlighting its effectiveness in reducing youth recidivism.

Case Study 2: Adult Restorative Justice Circles

Background:

- A restorative justice program for adult offenders focused on serious offenses, including assault and theft.

Methodology:

- Data Collection: Tracked reoffending rates using official records and self-reports.

- Longitudinal Study: Follow-up assessments conducted at one year, three years, and five years post-intervention.

- Comparative Analysis: Compared outcomes with a control group of adult offenders processed through the traditional justice system.

Findings:

- Lower Recidivism: The program achieved a 25% lower recidivism rate among participants compared to the control group.

- Long-Term Impact: Longitudinal data showed sustained reductions in reoffending rates over five years.

- Influential Factors: Key factors influencing lower recidivism included the quality of facilitation and the inclusion of community service components.

Impact:

- The program's success led to increased support from policymakers and the broader implementation of restorative justice circles for adult offenders.

Best Practices for Tracking Recidivism

Comprehensive Data Collection

Ensure comprehensive and accurate data collection:

- Multiple Sources: Use multiple data sources, including official records and self-reports, to capture a complete picture of recidivism.

- Standardized Measures: Employ standardized measures and definitions of recidivism to ensure consistency and comparability.

Regular Follow-Up

Conduct regular follow-up assessments to monitor long-term outcomes:

- Consistent Intervals: Schedule follow-up assessments at consistent intervals (e.g., annually) to track changes over time.

- Longitudinal Tracking: Maintain longitudinal tracking to understand the sustained impact of restorative justice interventions.

Contextual Analysis

Perform contextual analysis to understand the broader factors influencing recidivism:

- Demographic Insights: Analyze recidivism data by demographic factors to identify and address disparities.

- Program Elements: Evaluate the effectiveness of specific program elements to identify best practices and areas for improvement.

Tracking recidivism rates is a vital quantitative measure for assessing the effectiveness of restorative justice programs. By collecting accurate data, conducting longitudinal studies, and performing comparative analyses, practitioners can gain valuable insights into the long-term impact of restorative justice on reoffending rates. These insights are crucial for enhancing program effectiveness, justifying funding and support, and promoting the broader adoption of restorative justice practices. By implementing best practices for tracking and analyzing recidivism, restorative justice programs can create meaningful and lasting outcomes for participants and communities. As we continue to explore the measurement of restorative justice impact in this book, the insights gained from recidivism data will inform our broader discussion on creating effective and responsive restorative justice initiatives.

Quantitative Measures

Satisfaction Surveys: Measuring Participant Satisfaction with the Process

Participant satisfaction is a critical indicator of the success and impact of restorative justice programs. Satisfaction surveys provide valuable quantitative data on how participants perceive the process, including its fairness, effectiveness, and emotional impact. This chapter explores the importance of satisfaction surveys, methods for designing and administering them, analyzing the results, and using the insights to improve restorative justice programs.

Importance of Satisfaction Surveys

Assessing Program Quality

Satisfaction surveys help assess the quality of restorative justice programs:

- Participant Experience: They capture participants' experiences and perceptions, providing insights into the strengths and weaknesses of the program.

- Service Delivery: Feedback from satisfaction surveys can highlight areas where the service delivery needs improvement, ensuring that the program meets the needs of all participants.

Enhancing Participant Engagement

Understanding participant satisfaction can enhance engagement and commitment:

- Positive Reinforcement: High satisfaction levels reinforce the value of the restorative justice process for participants, encouraging their continued engagement.

- Trust and Confidence: Satisfied participants are more likely to trust the process and feel confident in its fairness and effectiveness.

Informing Program Development

Satisfaction surveys provide data that can inform the development and refinement of restorative justice programs:

- Continuous Improvement: Regularly collecting and analyzing satisfaction data allows for continuous improvement of the program.

- Participant-Centered Adjustments: Insights from satisfaction surveys guide adjustments that better align the program with participants' needs and expectations.

Designing Satisfaction Surveys

Key Elements of Effective Surveys

Effective satisfaction surveys should include several key elements:

- Clear and Concise Questions: Questions should be clear, concise, and easy to understand to ensure accurate responses.

- Balanced Format: Surveys should include a mix of quantitative and qualitative questions to capture a broad range of feedback.

Example Survey Questions:

- How satisfied were you with the overall restorative justice process?

- How well did the facilitator manage the sessions?

- Did you feel heard and respected during the process?

- What aspects of the process did you find most helpful?

- What suggestions do you have for improving the program?

Types of Questions

Incorporate various types of questions to capture comprehensive feedback:

- Likert Scale Questions: Use Likert scale questions (e.g., strongly agree, agree, neutral, disagree, strongly disagree) to measure satisfaction levels on different aspects of the process.

- Open-Ended Questions: Include open-ended questions to allow participants to provide detailed feedback and suggestions.

- Demographic Questions: Collect demographic information to analyze satisfaction across different participant groups.

Survey Administration Methods

Choose appropriate methods for administering satisfaction surveys:

- Paper Surveys: Distribute paper surveys during or after sessions for immediate feedback.

- Online Surveys: Use online survey tools to reach participants who prefer digital formats.

- Phone Interviews: Conduct phone interviews for participants who may have limited access to written or online surveys.

Administering Satisfaction Surveys

Timing of Surveys

Administer surveys at appropriate times to capture relevant feedback:

- Post-Session Surveys: Distribute surveys immediately after sessions to capture participants' initial reactions.

- Follow-Up Surveys: Conduct follow-up surveys several weeks or months after the process to assess long-term satisfaction and impact.

Encouraging Participation

Encourage high response rates to ensure comprehensive feedback:

- Anonymity: Guarantee anonymity to make participants feel comfortable providing honest feedback.

- Incentives: Offer incentives, such as gift cards or participation certificates, to encourage survey completion.

- Communication: Clearly communicate the purpose of the survey and how the feedback will be used to improve the program.

Analyzing Survey Results

Quantitative Analysis

Analyze quantitative data to identify trends and patterns:

- Descriptive Statistics: Calculate mean, median, and mode for Likert scale questions to summarize satisfaction levels.

- Comparative Analysis: Compare satisfaction levels across different demographic groups or over time to identify trends.

Example Analysis:

- Overall Satisfaction: Calculate the average satisfaction score for the overall process.

- Facilitator Performance: Analyze ratings for facilitator performance to identify strengths and areas for improvement.

- Respect and Inclusion: Measure satisfaction with how participants felt heard and respected during the process.

Qualitative Analysis

Analyze qualitative data to gain deeper insights:

- Thematic Analysis: Identify common themes and patterns in responses to open-ended questions.

- Content Analysis: Examine the frequency and context of specific words or phrases to understand participants' key concerns and suggestions.

Using Insights to Improve Programs

Identifying Areas for Improvement

Use survey results to identify specific areas for improvement:

- Targeted Adjustments: Make targeted adjustments to the program based on identified weaknesses or participant suggestions.

- Training Needs: Address training needs for facilitators or staff based on feedback about their performance.

Enhancing Strengths

Leverage positive feedback to enhance program strengths:

- Best Practices: Identify and reinforce best practices that contribute to high satisfaction levels.

- Program Promotion: Use positive feedback in promotional materials to highlight the program's successes and attract new participants.

Continuous Monitoring and Feedback Loops

Implement continuous monitoring and feedback loops to ensure ongoing improvement:

- Regular Surveys: Administer satisfaction surveys regularly to monitor changes and trends over time.

- Feedback Integration: Integrate feedback into program planning and development to ensure that participant needs and expectations are consistently met.

Case Studies

Case Study 1: Restorative Justice in Schools

Background:

- A restorative justice program implemented in a high school to address bullying and conflict.

Survey Design:

- Mixed-format survey with Likert scale questions and open-ended questions.

- Administered post-session and at the end of the school year.

Findings:

- High satisfaction with the facilitation of restorative circles.

- Positive feedback on the sense of inclusion and respect during the process.

- Suggestions for more follow-up sessions and additional training for peer facilitators.

Impact:

- Program adjustments included increased follow-up sessions and enhanced training for student facilitators.

- The school reported improved relationships and a reduction in bullying incidents.

Case Study 2: Community Restorative Justice Program

Background:

- A community-based restorative justice program addressing neighborhood conflicts.

Survey Design:

- Online surveys with a mix of quantitative and qualitative questions.

- Follow-up surveys conducted six months after the process.

Findings:

- High overall satisfaction with the program, particularly with the inclusivity and fairness of the process.

- Requests for more community involvement and support resources post-process.

Impact:

- The program expanded community involvement initiatives and introduced additional support resources.

- The community reported increased trust and collaboration among residents.

Best Practices for Satisfaction Surveys

Clear and Accessible Design

Ensure surveys are clear, concise, and accessible:

- User-Friendly Format: Design surveys that are easy to understand and complete.

- Multiple Languages: Offer surveys in multiple languages to accommodate diverse participants.

Regular Review and Adaptation

Regularly review and adapt surveys to keep them relevant and effective:

- Survey Updates: Update survey questions periodically to reflect evolving program aspects and participant needs.

- Feedback Utilization: Use survey results to make continuous improvements to the program.

Satisfaction surveys are a vital tool for measuring participant satisfaction with restorative justice processes. By designing effective surveys, administering them appropriately, and analyzing the results, practitioners can gain valuable insights into participants' experiences and perceptions. These insights are crucial for assessing program quality, enhancing participant engagement, and informing continuous improvement. Implementing best practices for satisfaction surveys ensures that restorative justice programs remain responsive to participants' needs and effective in achieving their goals. As we continue to explore the measurement of restorative justice impact in this book, the insights gained from satisfaction surveys will inform our broader discussion on creating successful and impactful restorative justice initiatives.

Long-term Outcomes

Sustained Behavior Changes: Monitoring Long-Term Behavior Changes in Offenders

Assessing the long-term impact of restorative justice involves monitoring sustained behavior changes in offenders. This chapter explores the importance of tracking long-term behavior changes, the methods for doing so, analyzing the data, and using the insights to enhance restorative justice programs. Understanding sustained behavior changes is crucial for determining the true effectiveness and transformative potential of restorative justice interventions.

Importance of Monitoring Long-Term Behavior Changes

Indicators of True Rehabilitation

Sustained behavior changes are key indicators of true rehabilitation and the effectiveness of restorative justice programs:

- Long-Term Success: Long-term behavior changes signify that the offender has internalized the lessons from the restorative justice process and is committed to a positive path.

- Reduction in Recidivism: Persistent changes in behavior are often correlated with lower recidivism rates, indicating successful rehabilitation.

Enhancing Community Safety

Tracking behavior changes contributes to enhancing community safety:

- Preventing Future Offenses: Sustained behavior change reduces the likelihood of future offenses, thereby increasing overall community safety.

- Building Trust: Demonstrating long-term behavior improvements helps build trust between the offender and the community.

Informing Policy and Practice

Monitoring long-term outcomes informs policy and practice:

- Evidence-Based Decisions: Long-term data provides evidence to support the effectiveness of restorative justice, guiding policy decisions and program funding.

- Program Refinement: Insights into sustained behavior changes help refine restorative justice practices to enhance their effectiveness.

Methods for Monitoring Sustained Behavior Changes

Longitudinal Studies

Longitudinal studies are essential for tracking behavior changes over extended periods:

- Baseline Measurement: Establish a baseline of offender behavior prior to the restorative justice intervention.

- Regular Follow-Ups: Conduct regular follow-ups at intervals such as six months, one year, two years, and five years to assess behavior changes.

Example Study Design:

- Cohort Selection: Select a cohort of offenders who have completed the restorative justice program.

- Control Group: Include a control group of similar offenders who did not participate in the program for comparative analysis.

- Data Points: Track various data points such as employment status, engagement in community activities, and any new offenses.

Self-Reports and Interviews

Collecting self-reports and conducting interviews provide qualitative insights into behavior changes:

- Self-Assessment Surveys: Administer self-assessment surveys where offenders report on their behavior, attitudes, and lifestyle changes.

- In-Depth Interviews: Conduct in-depth interviews to explore the offenders' perspectives on their behavior changes and the factors contributing to these changes.

Example Questions:

- How has your behavior changed since participating in the restorative justice program?

- What factors have influenced your ability to maintain these changes?

- Have you faced any challenges in sustaining positive behavior changes?

Third-Party Observations

Incorporate third-party observations for an objective assessment of behavior changes:

- Family and Community Feedback: Gather feedback from family members, employers, community leaders, and probation officers on the offender's behavior and integration into the community.

- Professional Assessments: Use assessments from social workers, counselors, or psychologists who have worked with the offender post-intervention.

Data Integration

Integrate data from multiple sources to get a comprehensive view of behavior changes:

- Combining Quantitative and Qualitative Data: Use both quantitative measures (e.g., recidivism rates) and qualitative insights (e.g., self-reports, interviews) for a holistic assessment.

- Longitudinal Tracking Systems: Implement tracking systems that compile data from various sources over time.

Analyzing Behavior Change Data

Quantitative Analysis

Analyze quantitative data to identify trends and patterns in behavior changes:

- Descriptive Statistics: Calculate descriptive statistics to summarize data points such as recidivism rates, employment rates, and community engagement.

- Comparative Analysis: Compare data between the cohort of restorative justice participants and the control group to identify significant differences.

Example Metrics:

- Recidivism Rates: Percentage of offenders who reoffend within specified time frames.

- Employment Status: Percentage of offenders who gain and maintain employment post-intervention.

- Community Engagement: Level of involvement in community activities or volunteer work.

Qualitative Analysis

Analyze qualitative data to gain deeper insights into behavior changes:

- Thematic Analysis: Identify common themes and factors that contribute to sustained behavior changes, such as support systems, personal motivations, and challenges faced.

- Narrative Analysis: Explore personal stories to understand the lived experiences and transformative processes of offenders.

Case Studies

Case Study 1: Restorative Justice for Youth Offenders

Background:

- A restorative justice program aimed at reducing recidivism among youth offenders involved in minor crimes.

Methodology:

- Longitudinal Study: Tracked behavior changes over five years with regular follow-ups.

- Self-Reports and Interviews: Collected self-reports and conducted in-depth interviews with participants and their families.

- Third-Party Observations: Gathered feedback from teachers, counselors, and community leaders.

Findings:

- Significant Behavior Change: A majority of participants showed significant positive behavior changes, including improved school attendance and reduced involvement in criminal activities.

- Key Factors: Factors contributing to sustained behavior changes included strong family support, engagement in positive community activities, and ongoing mentorship.

Impact:

- The program's success in achieving long-term behavior changes led to its expansion and increased funding, highlighting its effectiveness in rehabilitating youth offenders.

Case Study 2: Restorative Circles for Adult Offenders

Background:

- A restorative justice program using restorative circles for adult offenders involved in serious crimes, such as assault and theft.

Methodology:

- Longitudinal Study: Monitored behavior changes over five years with periodic follow-up assessments.

- Professional Assessments: Used assessments from social workers and probation officers.

- Community Feedback: Collected feedback from family members, employers, and community members.

Findings:

- Lower Recidivism Rates: Participants demonstrated lower recidivism rates compared to the control group.

- Sustained Employment: A significant number of participants maintained stable employment and reported positive community integration.

- Support Systems: The presence of robust support systems, such as counseling and community programs, was crucial for sustained behavior change.

Impact:

- The program's demonstrated ability to foster long-term behavior changes strengthened its credibility and led to broader implementation across the region.

Best Practices for Monitoring Sustained Behavior Changes

Comprehensive Data Collection

Ensure comprehensive and accurate data collection:

- Multiple Data Sources: Use multiple data sources, including self-reports, third-party observations, and official records, to capture a complete picture of behavior changes.

- Consistent Follow-Up: Conduct consistent follow-up assessments to track behavior changes over time.

Participant Engagement

Engage participants in the monitoring process to ensure accurate and meaningful data:

- Regular Check-Ins: Maintain regular check-ins with participants to monitor their progress and provide ongoing support.

- Encouraging Honesty: Create an environment that encourages honest self-reporting and open communication.

Integration of Support Services

Integrate support services to facilitate sustained behavior changes:

- Ongoing Counseling: Provide ongoing counseling and mentorship to help participants navigate challenges and maintain positive behavior changes.

- Community Programs: Connect participants with community programs that offer support, resources, and positive engagement opportunities.

Monitoring sustained behavior changes is essential for assessing the long-term impact of restorative justice programs. By employing methods such as longitudinal studies, self-reports, interviews, and third-party observations, practitioners can gain valuable insights into the effectiveness of these interventions. Analyzing this data helps identify the factors that contribute to successful behavior change and informs continuous improvement of restorative justice practices. By implementing best practices for tracking and analyzing behavior changes, restorative justice programs can achieve meaningful and lasting outcomes for offenders and communities. As we continue to explore the measurement of restorative justice impact in this book, the insights gained from monitoring sustained behavior changes will inform our broader discussion on creating effective and responsive restorative justice initiatives.

Community Impact: Evaluating the Broader Impact on Community Cohesion and Safety

Evaluating the broader impact of restorative justice on community cohesion and safety is essential for understanding the full scope of its benefits. This chapter explores the importance of community impact assessment, methods for evaluating this impact, analyzing the data, and using insights to enhance restorative justice programs. By focusing on community-level outcomes, restorative justice can be better understood and appreciated as a holistic approach to justice that benefits not only individuals but entire communities.

Importance of Community Impact Assessment

Enhancing Community Cohesion

Restorative justice aims to repair harm and rebuild relationships, which can significantly enhance community cohesion:

- Rebuilding Trust: Successful restorative justice processes can restore trust between community members, including victims, offenders, and their families.

- Strengthening Relationships: By involving the community in the justice process, relationships are strengthened, fostering a sense of solidarity and mutual support.

Improving Community Safety

Community safety is a primary concern addressed by restorative justice:

- Reducing Recidivism: By addressing the root causes of criminal behavior and facilitating rehabilitation, restorative justice helps reduce recidivism, leading to safer communities.

- Preventing Crime: Engaging community members in restorative justice can help prevent crime through increased vigilance and mutual accountability.

Informing Policy and Practice

Understanding the community impact of restorative justice informs policy and practice:

- Evidence-Based Advocacy: Demonstrating positive community outcomes can support advocacy for broader implementation of restorative justice practices.

- Program Development: Insights from community impact assessments help refine and improve restorative justice programs to better serve communities.

Methods for Evaluating Community Impact

Surveys and Questionnaires

Surveys and questionnaires can gather quantitative data on community perceptions and experiences:

- Community Surveys: Administer surveys to community members to assess their perceptions of safety, cohesion, and trust before and after the implementation of restorative justice programs.

- Targeted Questionnaires: Use targeted questionnaires to gather specific feedback from participants involved in restorative justice processes.

Example Survey Questions:

- How safe do you feel in your community?

- To what extent do you trust your neighbors and community members?

- How effective do you believe the restorative justice program has been in addressing community conflicts?

Focus Groups and Community Meetings

Focus groups and community meetings provide qualitative insights into the broader impact of restorative justice:

- Focus Groups: Conduct focus groups with diverse community members to discuss their experiences and perceptions of the restorative justice program.

- Community Meetings: Hold community meetings to gather feedback, encourage dialogue, and build consensus on the program's impact.

Example Discussion Topics:

- Changes in community relationships and trust levels.

- Perceived changes in community safety and crime rates.

- Suggestions for improving the restorative justice program.

Crime and Safety Statistics

Analyzing crime and safety statistics provides objective data on community impact:

- Crime Rates: Monitor changes in crime rates in the community before and after the implementation of restorative justice programs.

- Recidivism Data: Track recidivism rates to assess the long-term impact on community safety.

Example Metrics:

- Number of reported crimes.

- Types of crimes committed.

- Frequency of repeat offenses.

Case Studies and Narrative Analysis

Case studies and narrative analysis offer in-depth understanding of the community impact:

- Detailed Case Studies: Develop detailed case studies of specific incidents or conflicts addressed through restorative justice, highlighting the broader community impact.

- Narrative Analysis: Collect and analyze personal stories from community members to capture the qualitative impact of restorative justice.

Analyzing Community Impact Data

Quantitative Analysis

Analyze quantitative data to identify trends and measure impact:

- Descriptive Statistics: Calculate descriptive statistics to summarize survey responses and crime data.

- Comparative Analysis: Compare crime and safety statistics before and after the implementation of restorative justice programs.

Example Analysis:

- Changes in Perceived Safety: Measure changes in community members' perceptions of safety over time.

- Crime Rate Trends: Analyze trends in crime rates to determine the impact of restorative justice on community safety.

Qualitative Analysis

Analyze qualitative data to gain deeper insights into community impact:

- Thematic Analysis: Identify common themes and patterns in focus group discussions and narrative data.

- Content Analysis: Examine the frequency and context of specific words or phrases related to community cohesion and safety.

Case Studies

Case Study 1: Urban Community Restorative Justice Program

Background:

- An urban community implemented a restorative justice program to address conflicts and reduce crime.

Evaluation Methods:

- Community Surveys: Administered surveys to community members before and after the program's implementation.

- Focus Groups: Conducted focus groups with community leaders, victims, offenders, and residents.

Findings:

- Increased Trust: Surveys showed a significant increase in trust among community members.

- Reduced Crime Rates: Crime statistics indicated a 20% reduction in reported crimes after the program's implementation.

- Positive Feedback: Focus groups revealed positive feedback regarding the program's ability to resolve conflicts and enhance community relationships.

Impact:

- The program's success in improving community cohesion and safety led to its expansion to other urban areas.

Case Study 2: Rural Community Restorative Circles

Background:

- A rural community used restorative circles to address local disputes and enhance community cohesion.

Evaluation Methods:

- Community Meetings: Held community meetings to gather feedback and discuss the program's impact.

- Crime Data Analysis: Analyzed local crime data before and after the program's implementation.

Findings:

- Strengthened Relationships: Community meetings revealed strengthened relationships and increased mutual support among residents.

- Lower Recidivism Rates: Analysis showed a decrease in repeat offenses among participants in the restorative circles.

- Improved Perceptions of Safety: Residents reported feeling safer and more connected to their community.

Impact:

- The positive outcomes encouraged continued use of restorative circles and increased community engagement in the justice process.

Best Practices for Evaluating Community Impact

Comprehensive Data Collection

Ensure comprehensive data collection to capture a full picture of community impact:

- Multiple Methods: Use multiple methods, including surveys, focus groups, crime statistics, and narrative analysis, to gather diverse data.

- Regular Monitoring: Conduct regular monitoring to track changes and trends over time.

Inclusive Participation

Engage a broad range of community members in the evaluation process:

- Diverse Voices: Ensure that feedback is collected from a diverse range of community members, including those directly and indirectly affected by the program.

- Accessible Methods: Use accessible methods for data collection to ensure broad participation.

Transparent Reporting

Provide transparent reporting of findings to the community:

- Clear Communication: Communicate findings clearly and regularly to the community, highlighting both successes and areas for improvement.

- Feedback Integration: Integrate community feedback into program adjustments and development.

Evaluating the broader impact of restorative justice on community cohesion and safety is essential for understanding its full benefits and effectiveness. By using methods such as surveys, focus groups, crime data analysis, and narrative analysis, practitioners can gain comprehensive insights into the community-level outcomes of restorative justice programs. These insights are crucial for enhancing program effectiveness, building community trust, and informing policy and practice. Implementing best practices for evaluating community impact ensures that restorative justice programs are responsive to the needs of the community and effective in promoting long-term safety and cohesion. As we continue to explore the measurement of restorative justice impact in this book, the insights gained from community impact assessments will inform our broader discussion on creating successful and impactful restorative justice initiatives.

CHAPTER 09

FUTURE DIRECTIONS FOR RESTORATIVE JUSTICE

Policy Recommendations

Legislative Support: Advocating for Laws and Policies that Support Restorative Practices

Introduction

Legislative support is crucial for the widespread adoption and effectiveness of restorative justice. By advocating for laws and policies that support restorative practices, governments can institutionalize these approaches, ensuring they are accessible, sustainable, and integrated into the broader justice system. This chapter explores the importance of legislative support, strategies for advocating for supportive legislation, and examples of successful legislative initiatives.

Importance of Legislative Support

Institutionalizing Restorative Justice

Legislative support helps to institutionalize restorative justice practices within the legal system:

- Formal Recognition: Laws that formally recognize restorative justice validate its importance and legitimacy as an alternative to traditional justice processes.

- Sustainability: Legislation provides a sustainable framework for restorative justice, ensuring it is not dependent on temporary funding or pilot programs.

Ensuring Access and Equity

Supportive legislation ensures that restorative justice is accessible and equitable for all:

- Equal Access: Laws can mandate equal access to restorative justice programs for all individuals, regardless of their background or the nature of their offense.

- Fair Implementation: Legislation can establish guidelines and standards to ensure that restorative justice practices are implemented fairly and consistently.

Promoting Best Practices

Legislative support can promote the adoption of best practices in restorative justice:

- Standards and Guidelines: Laws can establish standards and guidelines for restorative justice programs, ensuring they adhere to best practices and are effective.

- Training and Education: Legislation can mandate training and education for practitioners, ensuring they have the necessary skills and knowledge to facilitate restorative processes effectively.

Strategies for Advocating for Supportive Legislation

Building Coalitions

Building coalitions with various stakeholders is essential for advocating for restorative justice legislation:

- Community Organizations: Partner with community organizations that have a vested interest in restorative justice, such as victim support groups, advocacy organizations, and educational institutions.

- Legal and Judicial Support: Engage legal and judicial professionals, including judges, lawyers, and law enforcement officials, to gain their support and expertise.

Example Coalition Members:

- Victim advocacy groups

- Criminal justice reform organizations

- Educational institutions and researchers

- Law enforcement agencies

- Legal professionals and bar associations

Educating Legislators

Educating legislators about the benefits and effectiveness of restorative justice is crucial:

- Informational Briefings: Organize informational briefings and workshops to educate legislators about restorative justice, its principles, and its positive outcomes.

- Research and Data: Provide legislators with research, data, and case studies that demonstrate the effectiveness of restorative justice in reducing recidivism, improving victim satisfaction, and enhancing community cohesion.

Key Points for Legislator Education:

- Restorative justice reduces recidivism rates and promotes rehabilitation.

- Victims report higher satisfaction with restorative justice compared to traditional justice processes.

- Restorative justice enhances community cohesion and safety.

Drafting and Proposing Legislation

Drafting and proposing legislation that supports restorative justice involves several key steps:

- Research and Drafting: Collaborate with legal experts to draft legislation that outlines the principles, standards, and implementation guidelines for restorative justice programs.

- Legislative Champions: Identify and work with legislative champions who are committed to restorative justice and can advocate for the proposed legislation within the legislative body.

Example Legislative Provisions:

- Establishment of restorative justice programs for specific offenses (e.g., juvenile offenses, non-violent crimes).

- Mandatory training and certification for restorative justice facilitators.

- Funding allocations for restorative justice program implementation and evaluation.

Engaging the Public

Public support is essential for advancing legislative initiatives:

- Public Awareness Campaigns: Launch public awareness campaigns to educate the public about restorative justice and garner widespread support.

- Grassroots Advocacy: Mobilize grassroots advocacy efforts, encouraging community members to contact their legislators and express support for restorative justice legislation.

Public Engagement Strategies:

- Social media campaigns highlighting success stories and benefits of restorative justice.

- Public forums and town hall meetings to discuss restorative justice and gather community input.

- Petition drives and letter-writing campaigns to demonstrate public support to legislators.

Examples of Successful Legislative Initiatives

New Zealand: The Children, Young Persons, and Their Families Act 1989

Overview:

- The Children, Young Persons, and Their Families Act 1989 in New Zealand is a landmark piece of legislation that integrates restorative justice principles into the youth justice system.

Key Provisions:

- Family Group Conferences (FGCs): The Act established FGCs as a key mechanism for addressing youth offenses, involving the young person, their family, victims, and community representatives in the decision-making process.

- Focus on Rehabilitation: The Act emphasizes rehabilitation and reintegration of young offenders into their communities, rather than punitive measures.

Impact:

- Reduced Recidivism: FGCs have been effective in reducing recidivism rates among young offenders.

- High Satisfaction: Victims and families report high levels of satisfaction with the restorative justice process.

Canada: The Youth Criminal Justice Act (YCJA) 2003

Overview:

- The Youth Criminal Justice Act (YCJA) in Canada incorporates restorative justice principles into the youth justice system.

Key Provisions:

- Extrajudicial Measures: The YCJA encourages the use of extrajudicial measures, such as restorative justice programs, for minor offenses.

- Victim Involvement: The Act promotes the involvement of victims in the justice process, emphasizing the need for reparative actions by young offenders.

Impact:

- Diversion from Court: The YCJA has successfully diverted many young offenders from the formal court system to restorative justice programs.

- Community Safety: The Act has contributed to enhanced community safety by addressing the root causes of criminal behavior.

Best Practices for Legislative Advocacy

Comprehensive Research and Data Collection

Ensure that legislative advocacy is informed by comprehensive research and data:

- Evidence-Based Proposals: Base legislative proposals on solid evidence demonstrating the effectiveness of restorative justice.

- Impact Assessments: Conduct impact assessments to predict the potential benefits and challenges of proposed legislation.

Continuous Engagement and Follow-Up

Maintain continuous engagement with legislators and stakeholders:

- Regular Updates: Provide regular updates to legislators on the progress and outcomes of restorative justice programs.

- Feedback Mechanisms: Establish feedback mechanisms to gather input from stakeholders and community members on the implementation of restorative justice legislation.

Adapting to Local Contexts

Tailor legislative proposals to the specific needs and contexts of local communities:

- Contextual Analysis: Conduct a thorough analysis of the local legal, social, and cultural context to ensure that proposed legislation is relevant and effective.

\- Community Involvement: Involve local communities in the drafting and advocacy process to ensure their needs and perspectives are addressed.

Legislative support is crucial for the widespread adoption and effectiveness of restorative justice. By advocating for laws and policies that support restorative practices, governments can institutionalize restorative justice, ensuring it is accessible, sustainable, and integrated into the broader justice system. Effective advocacy involves building coalitions, educating legislators, drafting and proposing legislation, and engaging the public. Examples from New Zealand and Canada demonstrate the positive impact of legislative support on restorative justice. Implementing best practices for legislative advocacy ensures that restorative justice programs are supported by a robust legal framework, promoting their long-term success and impact. As we continue to explore future directions for restorative justice in this book, the insights gained from legislative support will inform our broader discussion on creating effective and sustainable restorative justice initiatives.

Funding and Resources: Ensuring Adequate Funding and Resources for Restorative Justice Programs

Adequate funding and resources are essential for the successful implementation and sustainability of restorative justice programs. This chapter explores the importance of securing funding and resources, strategies for obtaining and managing them, and examples of successful funding models. By ensuring that restorative justice programs are well-funded and resourced, communities can maximize their effectiveness and long-term impact.

Importance of Funding and Resources

Program Implementation

Sufficient funding is crucial for the effective implementation of restorative justice programs:

- Operational Costs: Covering operational costs such as staffing, training, facilities, and materials.

- Program Expansion: Facilitating the expansion of programs to reach more participants and address a broader range of offenses.

Quality and Effectiveness

Adequate resources ensure the quality and effectiveness of restorative justice programs:

- Training and Professional Development: Providing ongoing training and professional development for facilitators and staff.

- Evaluation and Improvement: Funding for program evaluation and continuous improvement to ensure that restorative justice practices are effective and responsive to participants' needs.

Sustainability

Securing stable and long-term funding is essential for the sustainability of restorative justice programs:

- Consistent Services: Ensuring that programs can provide consistent and reliable services over time.

- Innovation and Adaptation: Supporting the development of innovative approaches and the ability to adapt to changing circumstances and needs.

Strategies for Securing Funding and Resources

Government Funding

Government funding is a primary source of financial support for restorative justice programs:

- Legislative Appropriations: Advocate for legislative appropriations specifically designated for restorative justice initiatives.

- Grants and Subsidies: Apply for government grants and subsidies that support criminal justice reform, community safety, and rehabilitation programs.

Example Government Funding Sources:

- Department of Justice

- State and local government criminal justice agencies

- Public safety and community development grants

Private Sector and Philanthropic Support

Private sector and philanthropic organizations can provide substantial funding and resources:

- Corporate Sponsorships: Seek sponsorships from corporations that have a vested interest in community development and social justice.

- Foundation Grants: Apply for grants from foundations that support criminal justice reform, youth programs, and community initiatives.

Example Private Sector and Philanthropic Support:

- Corporate social responsibility (CSR) programs

- Foundations such as the MacArthur Foundation, Open Society Foundations, and local community foundations

Community-Based Fundraising

Community-based fundraising efforts can generate additional resources and engage the community:

- Fundraising Events: Organize events such as charity runs, benefit concerts, and community fairs to raise funds and awareness.

- Crowdfunding Campaigns: Launch online crowdfunding campaigns to solicit small donations from a broad audience.

Example Community-Based Fundraising Initiatives:

- Benefit dinners and silent auctions

- Online crowdfunding platforms like GoFundMe and Kickstarter

Partnerships and Collaborations

Forming partnerships and collaborations can enhance resource availability:

- Nonprofit Organizations: Partner with nonprofit organizations that have similar goals and can provide resources and expertise.

- Educational Institutions: Collaborate with universities and colleges for research support, intern programs, and educational resources.

Example Partnerships:

- Local nonprofits specializing in mediation and conflict resolution

- University criminal justice departments offering research and internship opportunities

Managing and Allocating Resources

Budget Planning and Management

Effective budget planning and management are essential for maximizing the impact of available resources:

- Detailed Budget Plans: Develop detailed budget plans that outline projected expenses and funding sources.

- Financial Oversight: Implement robust financial oversight and accountability mechanisms to ensure transparent and efficient use of funds.

Example Budget Categories:

- Staffing and training

- Facility and operational costs

- Program development and evaluation

- Community outreach and education

Prioritizing Resource Allocation

Prioritize resource allocation to address the most critical needs and maximize impact:

- Core Program Activities: Ensure that core program activities such as facilitation, training, and participant support are adequately funded.

- Innovation and Growth: Allocate resources for innovation and program growth to expand reach and enhance effectiveness.

Example Resource Allocation Priorities:

- Facilitator salaries and training

- Participant support services (e.g., counseling, transportation)

- Program evaluation and improvement initiatives

Monitoring and Evaluation

Regular monitoring and evaluation help ensure that resources are used effectively:

- Performance Metrics: Establish performance metrics to track the impact of funding on program outcomes.

- Continuous Improvement: Use evaluation results to inform continuous improvement efforts and adjust resource allocation as needed.

Example Performance Metrics:

- Participant satisfaction and feedback

- Recidivism rates and behavioral outcomes

- Community impact and engagement levels

Examples of Successful Funding Models

New Zealand: Government-Supported Restorative Justice

Overview:

- In New Zealand, restorative justice programs receive substantial government support, integrated into the broader criminal justice system.

Funding Sources:

- Government Funding: Legislative appropriations and grants from the Ministry of Justice.

- Partnerships: Collaborations with nonprofit organizations and community groups.

Impact:

- Sustained Programs: Stable and long-term funding has ensured the sustainability and expansion of restorative justice programs.

- Positive Outcomes: Consistent funding has contributed to positive outcomes, including reduced recidivism and high participant satisfaction.

United States: Community-Based Restorative Justice Programs

Overview:

- Several community-based restorative justice programs in the United States have successfully secured funding through diverse sources.

Funding Sources:

- Government Grants: Federal and state grants supporting criminal justice reform.

- Philanthropic Support: Grants from foundations such as the MacArthur Foundation and the Open Society Foundations.

- Community Fundraising: Local fundraising events and online crowdfunding campaigns.

Impact:

- Program Expansion: Diverse funding sources have enabled the expansion of restorative justice programs to reach more participants.

- Community Engagement: Community-based fundraising has increased local engagement and support for restorative justice initiatives.

Best Practices for Securing and Managing Funding

Building Strong Cases for Support

Build strong cases for support by demonstrating the effectiveness and impact of restorative justice programs:

- Evidence-Based Results: Use data and case studies to highlight positive outcomes and the program's value.

- Compelling Narratives: Share compelling narratives that illustrate the transformative impact of restorative justice on individuals and communities.

Diversifying Funding Sources

Diversify funding sources to enhance stability and reduce dependence on a single source:

- Multiple Streams: Seek funding from various sources, including government, private sector, philanthropic organizations, and community fundraising.

- Long-Term Partnerships: Establish long-term partnerships with key funders to ensure ongoing support.

Transparent Reporting and Accountability

Maintain transparency and accountability in the use of funds to build trust and credibility:

- Regular Reporting: Provide regular financial and programmatic reports to funders and stakeholders.

- Accountability Measures: Implement accountability measures such as audits and oversight committees to ensure proper use of resources.

Securing adequate funding and resources is essential for the successful implementation and sustainability of restorative justice programs. By leveraging government funding, private sector and philanthropic support, community-based fundraising, and partnerships, restorative justice initiatives can obtain the resources needed to thrive. Effective management and allocation of resources, along with regular monitoring and evaluation, ensure that programs remain impactful and responsive to community needs. Implementing best practices for securing and managing funding ensures that restorative justice programs are well-supported and positioned for long-term success. As we continue to explore future directions for restorative justice in this book, the insights gained from funding and resource strategies will inform our broader discussion on creating effective and sustainable restorative justice initiatives.

Integrating with Traditional Justice Systems

Hybrid Models: Combining Restorative and Retributive Justice Approaches

Restorative justice and retributive justice are often seen as distinct and separate approaches to addressing crime. However, combining elements of both into hybrid models can offer a more comprehensive and balanced justice system. This chapter explores the concept of hybrid models, their benefits, and practical examples, as well as strategies for effectively integrating restorative justice with traditional justice systems.

Understanding Hybrid Models

Definition and Principles

Hybrid models integrate restorative justice practices within the framework of traditional retributive justice systems:

- Restorative Elements: Focus on repairing harm, involving victims, offenders, and the community in the justice process.

- Retributive Elements: Maintain aspects of accountability and punishment to deter crime and uphold social order.

Key Principles:

- Balance: Striking a balance between accountability and rehabilitation.

- Flexibility: Offering a range of responses to crime that can be tailored to individual cases.

- Holistic Approach: Addressing both the immediate harm and the underlying causes of criminal behavior.

Benefits of Hybrid Models

Comprehensive Justice

Hybrid models provide a more comprehensive approach to justice by addressing multiple dimensions of crime:

- Accountability and Rehabilitation: Combining punishment with opportunities for offenders to make amends and rehabilitate.

- Victim and Community Involvement: Ensuring that victims' needs are met and that community relationships are repaired.

Enhanced Outcomes

Research indicates that hybrid models can lead to better outcomes for all stakeholders:

- Reduced Recidivism: Offenders who participate in restorative practices alongside traditional sanctions are less likely to reoffend.

- Victim Satisfaction: Victims report higher levels of satisfaction and a greater sense of closure when involved in restorative processes.

- Community Cohesion: Restorative elements help strengthen community bonds and reduce fear and mistrust.

Flexibility and Responsiveness

Hybrid models offer flexibility and can be more responsive to the needs of different cases:

- Tailored Responses: Allowing for tailored responses that consider the severity of the crime, the needs of the victim, and the potential for offender rehabilitation.

- Adapting to Contexts: Being adaptable to various legal, social, and cultural contexts, making justice systems more inclusive and effective.

Examples of Hybrid Models

New Zealand: Family Group Conferences within the Youth Justice System

Overview:

- In New Zealand, Family Group Conferences (FGCs) are integrated into the youth justice system, combining restorative practices with traditional legal processes.

Implementation:

- Restorative Element: FGCs involve the young offender, their family, victims, and community members in discussing the offense and agreeing on a plan for reparation and rehabilitation.

- Retributive Element: The outcomes of FGCs can be integrated into formal legal proceedings, and traditional sanctions can be applied if necessary.

Impact:

- Positive Outcomes: FGCs have led to reduced recidivism rates, high levels of victim satisfaction, and successful rehabilitation of young offenders.

- System Integration: The integration of FGCs within the legal framework ensures that restorative practices are supported and reinforced by the formal justice system.

Canada: Restorative Justice within Adult Probation

Overview:

- Some provinces in Canada have integrated restorative justice practices into adult probation services.

Implementation:

- Restorative Element: Offenders on probation can participate in restorative justice programs, such as victim-offender mediation or community circles, as part of their probation conditions.

- Retributive Element: Traditional probation conditions, such as reporting to a probation officer and adhering to curfews, are maintained.

Impact:

- Enhanced Rehabilitation: Combining restorative justice with probation has led to improved rehabilitation outcomes and reduced recidivism.

- Victim Engagement: Victims have the opportunity to be involved in the justice process and receive reparations.

United States: Restorative Practices in Sentencing

Overview:

- Some jurisdictions in the United States incorporate restorative justice practices into the sentencing phase of criminal proceedings.

Implementation:

- Restorative Element: Judges can order offenders to participate in restorative justice programs, such as victim-offender dialogues or community service, as part of their sentence.

- Retributive Element: Offenders still receive traditional sentences, such as incarceration or fines, alongside restorative obligations.

Impact:

- Balanced Approach: This approach ensures that offenders are held accountable while also addressing the harm caused and promoting rehabilitation.

- Community Benefits: Restorative sentencing can lead to stronger community relations and reduced crime rates.

Strategies for Effective Integration

Legal and Policy Frameworks

Developing supportive legal and policy frameworks is essential for integrating hybrid models:

- Legislation: Enact laws that formally recognize and support the use of restorative justice within the traditional justice system.

- Guidelines: Establish clear guidelines for how restorative practices can be integrated at various stages of the justice process.

Example Legal Provisions:

- Mandating the consideration of restorative justice options in sentencing.

- Providing for the use of restorative practices in probation and parole conditions.

Training and Education

Training and education for all stakeholders are crucial for the successful implementation of hybrid models:

- Judges and Lawyers: Provide training on the principles and practices of restorative justice and how they can be integrated with traditional legal processes.

- Law Enforcement: Educate police and probation officers on the benefits of restorative justice and their role in facilitating these practices.

- Community Members: Offer education and awareness programs to build community support and involvement.

Example Training Programs:

- Workshops and seminars on restorative justice for legal professionals.

- Community education sessions to explain the benefits and processes of restorative justice.

Collaborative Partnerships

Building collaborative partnerships enhances the integration of hybrid models:

- Interagency Collaboration: Foster collaboration between justice agencies, community organizations, and restorative justice practitioners.

- Community Involvement: Engage community members and organizations in the design and implementation of restorative justice programs.

Example Collaborative Initiatives:

- Joint training programs for police, probation officers, and restorative justice facilitators.

- Community advisory boards to guide the development and implementation of restorative justice practices.

Monitoring and Evaluation

Regular monitoring and evaluation are essential to assess the effectiveness of hybrid models:

- Performance Metrics: Establish metrics to measure the impact of hybrid models on recidivism, victim satisfaction, and community safety.

- Continuous Improvement: Use evaluation results to continuously improve the integration of restorative and retributive practices.

Example Evaluation Metrics:

- Recidivism rates among participants in hybrid models.

- Levels of victim satisfaction and sense of closure.

- Changes in community perceptions of safety and cohesion.

Hybrid models that combine restorative and retributive justice approaches offer a comprehensive and balanced response to crime. By integrating restorative practices within traditional justice systems, these models provide a flexible, responsive, and holistic approach to justice that benefits victims, offenders, and communities. Effective integration requires supportive legal and policy frameworks, training and education for all stakeholders, collaborative partnerships, and regular monitoring and evaluation. As we continue to explore future directions for restorative justice in this book, the insights gained from hybrid models will inform our broader discussion on creating effective and sustainable justice initiatives.

Collaborative Efforts: Encouraging Collaboration Between Restorative Justice Practitioners and Traditional Justice Professionals

Effective collaboration between restorative justice practitioners and traditional justice professionals is crucial for integrating restorative practices within the broader justice system. This chapter explores the importance of collaborative efforts, strategies for fostering collaboration, and examples of successful partnerships. By encouraging collaboration, restorative justice can be seamlessly incorporated into traditional justice processes, enhancing the overall effectiveness and reach of justice systems.

Importance of Collaborative Efforts

Holistic Approach to Justice

Collaboration between restorative and traditional justice professionals creates a more holistic approach to justice:

- Comprehensive Solutions: Combining the strengths of both approaches leads to more comprehensive solutions that address the needs of victims, offenders, and communities.

- Balanced Justice: Collaboration ensures a balance between accountability, rehabilitation, and community healing.

Enhanced Program Effectiveness

Collaborative efforts enhance the effectiveness of restorative justice programs:

- Resource Sharing: Sharing resources, knowledge, and expertise improves the quality and reach of restorative justice initiatives.

- Consistency: Collaboration promotes consistency in the application of restorative practices across different cases and contexts.

Increased Credibility and Acceptance

Collaborative efforts increase the credibility and acceptance of restorative justice within the traditional justice system:

- Legitimacy: Collaboration with traditional justice professionals lends legitimacy to restorative justice practices.

- Buy-In: Engaging traditional justice professionals fosters buy-in and support for restorative approaches.

Strategies for Fostering Collaboration

Building Relationships

Building strong relationships between restorative justice practitioners and traditional justice professionals is the foundation of effective collaboration:

- Networking: Facilitate networking opportunities through conferences, workshops, and professional associations.

- Regular Meetings: Hold regular interagency meetings to discuss cases, share updates, and plan collaborative initiatives.

Example Networking Initiatives:

- Joint conferences and seminars focused on restorative and traditional justice.

- Professional associations that include members from both fields.

Joint Training and Education

Joint training and education programs help bridge the gap between restorative and traditional justice approaches:

- Cross-Training: Provide cross-training programs where restorative justice practitioners and traditional justice professionals learn about each other's methods and practices.

- Continuing Education: Offer continuing education courses that cover the principles and benefits of restorative justice.

Example Training Programs:

- Workshops on integrating restorative practices into traditional legal processes.

- Training sessions on the benefits of restorative justice for judges, lawyers, and law enforcement officers.

Collaborative Case Management

Implementing collaborative case management practices ensures that restorative and traditional justice approaches are effectively integrated:

- Co-Case Management: Establish co-case management teams that include both restorative justice practitioners and traditional justice professionals.

- Joint Decision-Making: Facilitate joint decision-making processes for cases that could benefit from restorative justice interventions.

Example Case Management Practices:

- Co-facilitation of restorative justice processes by traditional justice professionals and restorative justice practitioners.

- Regular case review meetings to assess progress and make collaborative decisions.

Shared Resources and Infrastructure

Sharing resources and infrastructure supports the integration of restorative justice within traditional justice systems:

- Facilities: Use shared facilities for restorative justice meetings and traditional justice proceedings.

- Technology: Implement shared technology platforms for case management, communication, and data tracking.

Example Shared Resources:

- Community justice centers that house both restorative and traditional justice services.

- Integrated case management software that tracks restorative justice outcomes and traditional legal proceedings.

Policy and Protocol Development

Developing joint policies and protocols formalizes collaborative efforts:

- Memoranda of Understanding (MOUs): Establish MOUs between restorative justice organizations and traditional justice agencies to outline roles, responsibilities, and collaborative practices.

- Integrated Protocols: Develop integrated protocols that guide the use of restorative justice within traditional justice processes.

Example Policies and Protocols:

- MOUs that define how restorative justice can be used as a diversionary measure or as part of sentencing.

- Protocols for referring cases to restorative justice programs and tracking outcomes.

Examples of Successful Collaborative Efforts

United Kingdom: Restorative Justice in the Criminal Justice System

Overview:

- In the UK, restorative justice is integrated into the criminal justice system through collaborative efforts between restorative justice practitioners and traditional justice professionals.

Implementation:

- Joint Training: Regular joint training programs for police officers, probation officers, and restorative justice facilitators.

- Co-Case Management: Co-case management teams that work together on cases suitable for restorative justice interventions.

Impact:

- Positive Outcomes: High levels of victim satisfaction, reduced recidivism rates, and successful reintegration of offenders.

- System Integration: Strong collaboration has led to the seamless integration of restorative justice into the criminal justice system.

Canada: Community Justice Initiatives

Overview:

- Community justice initiatives in Canada involve collaboration between restorative justice organizations and traditional justice agencies to address local conflicts.

Implementation:

- Shared Facilities: Community justice centers that provide both restorative justice services and traditional legal assistance.

- Collaborative Protocols: Joint protocols for referring cases to restorative justice programs and monitoring outcomes.

Impact:

- Community Cohesion: Enhanced community cohesion and safety, with community members actively participating in the justice process.

- Comprehensive Justice: A more comprehensive approach to justice that addresses both legal and social dimensions of crime.

Best Practices for Encouraging Collaboration

Inclusive Planning and Development

Involve all relevant stakeholders in the planning and development of collaborative efforts:

- Stakeholder Engagement: Engage judges, lawyers, law enforcement, community leaders, and restorative justice practitioners in planning processes.

- Collaborative Development: Develop collaborative initiatives through inclusive and participatory processes.

Example Stakeholder Engagement:

- Planning committees that include representatives from all relevant sectors.

- Regular consultation meetings to gather input and build consensus.

Continuous Communication and Feedback

Maintain continuous communication and feedback loops between restorative and traditional justice professionals:

- Communication Channels: Establish formal communication channels, such as regular meetings, email lists, and collaborative platforms.

- Feedback Mechanisms: Implement feedback mechanisms to assess the effectiveness of collaboration and identify areas for improvement.

Example Communication Practices:

- Monthly interagency meetings to discuss ongoing cases and collaborative initiatives.

- Online forums or platforms for continuous dialogue and information sharing.

Evaluation and Adjustment

Regularly evaluate collaborative efforts and make necessary adjustments:

- Monitoring and Evaluation: Implement monitoring and evaluation frameworks to assess the impact of collaborative initiatives.

- Adaptive Management: Use evaluation findings to make data-driven adjustments and improvements to collaborative practices.

 Example Evaluation Metrics:

- Success rates of cases handled collaboratively.

- Satisfaction levels of victims, offenders, and professionals involved in collaborative efforts.

- Impact on recidivism and community safety.

Collaborative efforts between restorative justice practitioners and traditional justice professionals are essential for integrating restorative practices within the broader justice system. By building strong relationships, implementing joint training programs, adopting collaborative case management practices, sharing resources, and developing joint policies and protocols, restorative justice can be effectively combined with traditional justice approaches. Successful examples from the UK and Canada demonstrate the positive impact of such collaborations. Implementing best practices for encouraging collaboration ensures that restorative justice programs are supported, credible, and effective. As we continue to explore future directions for restorative justice in this book, the insights gained from collaborative efforts will inform our broader discussion on creating integrated and comprehensive justice initiatives.

CHAPTER 10

CONCLUSION

The Power and Promise of Restorative Justice

Restorative justice represents a transformative approach to addressing crime and conflict, offering a powerful alternative to traditional justice systems. By emphasizing healing, accountability, and community involvement, restorative justice circles provide profound psychological and emotional benefits for participants, contributing to both individual and communal well-being.

Psychological and Emotional Impacts

Restorative justice circles have significant psychological and emotional impacts on all participants:

- Empathy and Understanding: By facilitating direct communication between victims, offenders, and community members, restorative justice fosters empathy and understanding. Participants are encouraged to see beyond their own perspectives and recognize the humanity and experiences of others.

- Healing and Closure: For victims, restorative justice provides an opportunity to express their feelings, ask questions, and receive apologies. This process can be deeply healing, offering a sense of closure that is often absent in traditional justice proceedings.

- Accountability and Rehabilitation: Offenders are given the chance to take responsibility for their actions in a meaningful way, promoting genuine remorse and a commitment to change. This accountability is crucial for their rehabilitation and reintegration into society.

Benefits to Community and Society

Beyond individual impacts, restorative justice has broader benefits for communities and society:

- Reduced Recidivism: Studies have shown that participants in restorative justice programs are less likely to reoffend, leading to lower recidivism rates. This reduction in repeat offenses contributes to overall community safety.

- Strengthened Community Bonds: By involving community members in the justice process, restorative justice helps rebuild trust and strengthen social bonds. Communities become more resilient and cohesive, better equipped to address conflicts and support one another.

- Holistic Solutions: Restorative justice addresses the root causes of criminal behavior, promoting holistic solutions that consider the needs of victims, offenders, and the community. This comprehensive approach can lead to more sustainable and lasting outcomes.

Addressing Potential Risks

While restorative justice offers many benefits, it is crucial to address potential risks and challenges:

- Emotional Risks: Both victims and offenders may face emotional risks, such as re-traumatization or feelings of shame and guilt. Facilitators must be trained to manage these dynamics and provide appropriate support.

- Power Imbalances: Ensuring that all voices are heard and respected requires careful management of power imbalances. Skilled facilitators and inclusive practices are essential for creating a fair and equitable process.

- Consistency and Quality: Maintaining consistency and quality across restorative justice programs is vital. This requires ongoing training, monitoring, and evaluation to ensure that best practices are followed and that programs are effective.

Ensuring Support for Participants

Supporting all participants throughout the restorative justice process is critical for its success:

- Preparation and Follow-Up: Adequate preparation and follow-up are essential for helping participants navigate the process and integrate its outcomes. This includes pre-session counseling, ongoing support, and regular check-ins.

- Access to Resources: Providing access to resources such as counseling, legal advice, and community support services ensures that participants have the support they need to heal and move forward.

- Inclusive Practices: Ensuring that restorative justice practices are inclusive and culturally sensitive helps create a safe and supportive environment for all participants.

Future Directions

As we continue to explore and implement restorative practices, several key areas will shape the future of restorative justice:

- Legislative Support: Advocating for laws and policies that support restorative practices is crucial for their broader adoption and sustainability. Legislative support can provide the necessary framework and resources for effective implementation.

- Funding and Resources: Securing adequate funding and resources ensures that restorative justice programs can be implemented successfully and sustained over time. This includes government funding, private sector support, and community-based fundraising.

- Collaboration with Traditional Justice Systems: Encouraging collaboration between restorative justice practitioners and traditional justice professionals enhances the integration of restorative practices within the broader justice system. Hybrid models that combine restorative and retributive approaches can offer comprehensive solutions to crime and conflict.

Final Thoughts

Restorative justice holds immense promise as a powerful alternative to traditional justice systems. By fostering empathy, healing, and reduced recidivism, restorative justice circles contribute to the well-being of individuals and communities. As we continue to explore and implement restorative practices, it is crucial to address potential risks and ensure that all participants are supported throughout the process.

The journey towards a more just and compassionate society requires the collective effort of individuals, communities, and justice professionals. By embracing restorative justice, we can create a justice system that not only holds offenders accountable but also heals and restores the fabric of our communities. This holistic approach to justice, grounded in empathy and mutual respect, offers a path forward that prioritizes healing and transformation over punishment and retribution.

As we move forward, let us commit to fostering restorative justice practices that honor the dignity and humanity of all individuals, creating a foundation for lasting peace and justice in our communities.

REFERENCES

A comprehensive list of references, including academic articles, books, and case studies, will provide readers with additional resources to explore the topics covered in this book further. Below are the key sources that informed the content and discussions within this book.

Academic Articles

1. Braithwaite, J. (1989). Crime, Shame and Reintegration. Cambridge University Press.

2. Zehr, H. (2002). The Little Book of Restorative Justice. Good Books.

3. Latimer, J., Dowden, C., & Muise, D. (2005). The effectiveness of restorative justice practices: A meta-analysis. Prison Journal, 85(2), 127-144.

4. Sherman, L. W., & Strang, H. (2007). Restorative Justice: The Evidence. The Smith Institute.

5. Gavrielides, T. (2007). Restorative justice theory and practice: Addressing the discrepancy. European Institute for Crime Prevention and Control.

6. Daly, K. (2006). The limits of restorative justice. In Handbook of Restorative Justice (pp. 134-145). Routledge.

Books

1. Johnstone, G., & Van Ness, D. W. (Eds.). (2007). Handbook of Restorative Justice. Routledge.

2. Pranis, K., Stuart, B., & Wedge, M. (2003). Peacemaking Circles: From Crime to Community. Living Justice Press.

3. Umbreit, M. S., Vos, B., Coates, R. B., & Lightfoot, E. (2005). Restorative Justice in the Twenty-First Century: A Social Movement Full of Opportunities and Pitfalls. Marquette Law Review.

4. Zehr, H., & Toews, B. (Eds.). (2004). Critical Issues in Restorative Justice. Criminal Justice Press.

5. Van Ness, D. W., & Strong, K. H. (2014). Restoring Justice: An Introduction to Restorative Justice (5th ed.). Anderson Publishing.

6. Liebmann, M. (2007). Restorative Justice: How It Works. Jessica Kingsley Publishers.

Case Studies

1. Maxwell, G., & Morris, A. (2006). Youth justice in New Zealand: Restorative justice in practice. Journal of Social Issues, 62(2), 239-258.

2. McCold, P., & Wachtel, B. (2002). Restorative justice theory validation. In Restorative Justice for Juveniles: Conferencing, Mediation and Circles (pp. 110-142). Hart Publishing.

3. Office of Juvenile Justice and Delinquency Prevention (OJJDP). (2001). Family Group Conferencing: Implications for Crime Victims. U.S. Department of Justice.

4. Shapland, J., Robinson, G., & Sorsby, A. (2011). Restorative Justice in Practice: Evaluating What Works for Victims and Offenders. Routledge.

5. Van Ness, D. W. (2002). The shape of things to come: A framework for thinking about a restorative justice system. In Restorative Justice: Theoretical Foundations (pp. 1-20). Willan Publishing.

Reports and Papers

1. Department of Justice Canada. (2006). A Survey of Justice Practitioners on Restorative Justice. Research and Statistics Division.

2. New Zealand Ministry of Justice. (2016). Restorative Justice: Best Practice in New Zealand. Ministry of Justice.

3. Restorative Justice Council. (2015). Restorative Justice Works: Why It Matters and How It Can Be Done. Restorative Justice Council.

4. United Nations Office on Drugs and Crime (UNODC). (2006). Handbook on Restorative Justice Programmes. United Nations.

5. Canadian Resource Centre for Victims of Crime. (2011). Restorative Justice in Canada: What Victims Should Know. Canadian Resource Centre for Victims of Crime.

Online Resources

1. Restorative Justice Clearinghouse. (n.d.). Retrieved from www.restorativejustice.org

2. International Institute for Restorative Practices (IIRP). (n.d.). Retrieved from www.iirp.edu

3. Center for Justice & Reconciliation. (n.d.). Restorative Justice. Retrieved from www.restorativejustice.org

These references provide a robust foundation for further exploration into restorative justice, offering a range of perspectives from theoretical foundations to practical applications. By consulting these sources, readers can deepen their understanding of restorative justice and its profound impact on individuals and communities. As the field continues to evolve, staying informed through ongoing research and case studies will be essential for practitioners, policymakers, and scholars alike.